A SPIRITUAL JOURNEY INTO ECCLESIASTES

A SPIRITUAL JOURNEY INTO ECCLESIASTES

THE EYE OF GOD IS EVER UPON THOSE WHO LOVE HIM

LEON W. HOVISH

XULON PRESS

Xulon Press
2301 Lucien Way #415
Maitland, FL 32751
407.339.4217
www.xulonpress.com

© 2023 by Leon W. Hovish

All rights reserved solely by the author. The author guarantees all contents are original and do not infringe upon the legal rights of any other person or work. No part of this book may be reproduced in any form without the permission of the author.

Due to the changing nature of the Internet, if there are any web addresses, links, or URLs included in this manuscript, these may have been altered and may no longer be accessible. The views and opinions shared in this book belong solely to the author and do not necessarily reflect those of the publisher. The publisher therefore disclaims responsibility for the views or opinions expressed within the work.

Unless otherwise indicated, New American Bible For Catholics With Revised New Testament and Revised book of Psalms Printed by World Bible Publishers Inc. © Copyright 1970 By The Confraternity of Christian Doctrine, Washington D.C.

Paperback ISBN-13: 978-1-66286-998-3
Ebook ISBN-13: 978-1-66286-999-0

Contents

Foreword ix
Chapter 1 Vanity of Toil 1
Chapter 2 Study of Pleasure Seeking 11
Chapter 3 A Time for Every Affair 19
Chapter 4 Rivalry of One Man for Another 27
Chapter 5 Let Your Words be Few 45
Chapter 6 Limited Worth of Enjoyment 55
Chapter 7 Critque of Sages 61
Chapter 8 Who is Like the Wise Man 85
Chapter 9 Man Does Not know What is to Come 99
Chapter 10 When Hands are Lazy 117
Chapter 11 Cast Your Bread Upon the Waters 133
Chapter 12 Remember Your Creator 145
Chapter 13 My Personal Moment of Ecclesiastes 151
Photography Credits 159
About the Author 161

This book is first dedicated to the Triune God: Father, Son, and Holy Spirit. United as One they are the Alpha and Omega of my spiritual life. Without God's guidance and love this book would not have been possible.

I would also like to dedicate this book to my wife Peggy who managed to keep me on track day after day when my mind and desire wanted to wander elsewhere!

And finally I would like to dedicate this book to all seekers after God; may your searching for God bear the harvest of His real presence, wisdom and love in your life so that your life is not a vanity and a chase after wind and the God of Heaven and Earth remembers you always.

U.S. Copyright Office—Certification Registration No. TXu002299001

Foreword

ONE OF MY prized spiritual possessions is an old paperback Bible entitled: "The New American Bible for Catholics—With Revised New Testament and Revised Book of Psalms." It has an introduction by Pope Saint Paul VI and is dated September 18, 1970.

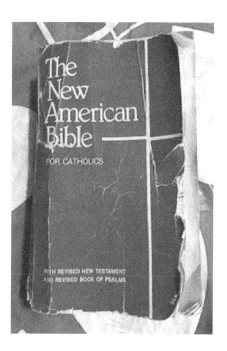

It is old and tattered, and I have repaired it so many times with Scotch tape that now the tape needs repair on occasion! It is riddled throughout with side comments I have written in pen and pencil as the Spirit moved me to react and comment on God's holy Word. I also underlined numerous sentences and phrases that caused either a spiritual or visceral reaction when I read them. I did not always agree with what was written, which surprised me to no end as I thought that the inspired Word of God through the prophets and saints would be so spiritually logical, that a spiritual person wouldn't be able to argue with them.

However, on occasion I did argue. Over the slow passage of time and experience, I would often see where my thought process was flawed, and I would eventually come to agreement with what was written. For some things I am still in disagreement even at the ripe old age of seventy. Some sections moved me to comment or underline key sentences and phrases more than others.

In the Old Testament, in the Wisdom books, I noticed I made more comments and underlined more phrases than in any of the Wisdom books or in most of the Old Testament books. In Ecclesiastes, chapter 3 titled: "Man Cannot Hit on the Right Time to Act," I took much solace and spiritual encouragement over the years. While this book discusses all twelve chapters of Ecclesiastes, it is chapter 3 that has made me appreciate the ancient wisdom of the Jewish priests, scribes, saints, and prophets who dedicated themselves to God and, through the inspiration of the Holy Spirit, wrote such wonderful words that I believe will last as long as humanity lasts and perhaps even beyond.

I am not a priest or monk, nor am I a trained theologian. I will probably not add anything new to the conversation that brighter minds and more spiritual people haven't already said. Yet each generation should have its say about their spiritual journey. I am not an expert on God. I am a spiritual journeyman seeking to deepen my connection to God through the only way He is allowing human beings to connect to Him: through faith, hope, and love. I hope and pray that you can see that attempt at spiritual communion in the words I've written.

If not, I can at least leave you with His inspired Word from chapter 3 of Ecclesiastes. May you always gain in wisdom, faith, hope, and love of and in Almighty God.

Foreword

"Man Cannot Hit on the Time to Act"
There is an appointed time for everything, and a time for every affair under the heavens.
A time to be born, and a time to die,
a time to plant, and a time to uproot the plant.
A time to kill, and a time to heal;
a time to tear down, and a time to build.
A time to weep, and a time to laugh;
a time to mourn, and a time to dance.
A time to scatter stones, and a time to gather them;
a time to embrace, and a time to be far from embraces.
A time to seek, and a time to lose;
a time to keep, and a time to cast away.
A time to rend, and a time to sew;
a time to be silent, and a time to speak.
A time to love, and a time to hate;
a time of war, and a time of peace.
What advantage has the worker from his toil? I have considered the task which God has appointed for men to be busied about. He has made everything appropriate to its time, and has put the timeless into their hearts, without men's ever discovering, from beginning to end, the work which God has done.
I recognize that there is nothing better than to be glad and to do well in life. For every man, moreover, to eat and drink and enjoy the fruit of all his labor is a gift of God. I recognize that whatever God does will endure forever; there is no adding to it, or taking from it. Thus has God done that he might be revered. What now is has already been; what is to be, already is; and God restores what otherwise would be displaced. (Eccles. 3:1–15)

Chapter 1

The structure of this book will take the form of various passages from Ecclesiastes in sequential order displayed first, and then a short honest discourse on my reactions and thoughts to those words follows. If, like me, you are a spiritual journalist, I encourage you to also write down your thoughts and feelings as the Spirit moves you to do so. I have found useful over the years, to read others' thoughts and feelings about their relationship with God. They tend to stimulate my own thinking and strengthen my own faith in God.

So let's begin:

"The words of David' son, Qoheleth, King in Jerusalem."
Vanity of Toil Without Profit
"Vanity of vanities, says Qoheleth, vanity of vanities! All things are vanity!
What profit has man from all his labor which he toils at under the sun?
One generation passes and another comes, but the world forever stays.
The sun rises and the sun goes down, then it presses on to the place where it rises.
Blowing now to the south, then toward the north, the wind turns again and again, resuming its rounds.
All rivers go to the sea, yet never does the sea become full. To the place where they go, the rivers keep on going." (Eccles. 1:1–7)

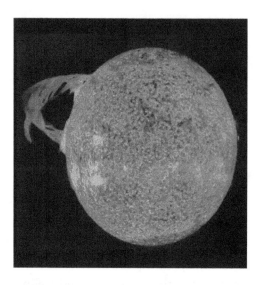

The previous passages have always spoken to me about the seeming permanence of the earth and sky when compared to man's impermanence on the face of the earth. It asks the tough question: "If we all pass away and our works and their results pass away too, of what good is it if none remember us or our works?" Although it does not state it explicitly, it points to the even deeper question of our true purpose and meaning in this life, if everything we do is only temporary. That is, why exist at all if our coming and passing is no different than the animals, fish and fowl of land, sea, and air?"

The bigger question of what is the meaning and purpose of mankind's existence will be discussed later on. Let us first discuss the value of one's labor. To me, the answer to the question of what does a man's labor profit him if no one remembers him is simple. Our labors are for the here and now. Our labor lends dignity to our lives whether we are remembered or not or even if they have no lasting effect on the people who come after us. Our labors provide a roof over our heads, clothes upon our persons, and food in our bellies. Our labors give us a sense of dignity and self-worth. Our labors give us a focus and purpose.

A life without focus and purpose is a life unmoored from our very sense of self. God has made this world in such a way that very few of us can get away with a lifetime of not having to work.

Chapter 1

Work Is a Gift, Not a Burden

Like Qoheleth, we too often wonder about the reason for our labor and its value, not only while we do it, but what effect it might have on others when we pass on? We all seek meaning and purpose in life and all of us, vanities of vanities, want to leave something of ourselves in passing. We want to be remembered as living and breathing beings, not as dust in the wind. Yet, eventually, that is what we become: dust in the wind. We no longer exist in this world when the last person to remember us also passes on to the next life. And that bothers us—greatly. The only satisfying answer must come through a leap of spiritual faith. It will not come through reason, or logic, or scientific discovery, or a creation by humankind. God Will Remember You Because:

> **"But as it is written: What eye has not seen, and ear has not heard, and what has not entered the human heart, what God has prepared for those who love Him." Corinthians 1-2:9**

For those of us who are immersed in the physicality of this world, the answer is unsatisfactory. We want to know in no uncertain circumstance that God will remember us. God does not give us that kind of "scientific" certainty. For the spiritual person, it is a hope, not knowledge of an afterlife. Scientific knowledge brings with it a certain amount of certainty based on observable facts from the physical world; hope on the other hand brings with it the fruit of faith.

So, like Qoheleth, both of us are stuck without knowing the answer, at least in terms of scientific knowing. So both of us wonder, does our existence and labor have purpose and meaning? Will anything we did or anything about us pass into eternity? Do we indeed toil for nothing; are all our efforts at the end of life for nothing? I do not think so, for my belief, my hope, and my faith is in a God who will remember me and who loves me, strengthens me, and helps me find purpose and meaning in my efforts. I do not despair over this life of mine; I take great joy in it! As Qoheleth says later, it is good for me to enjoy my labors and the fruit of my labors, to take my honest pleasures as I receive them—and so should you!

Qoheleth observes the more permanent nature of the greater physical world and seems to mourn that people (i.e., generations) come and go and share no permanence upon it. While I question why we have so short an existence and wonder from whence we came and where we will go after passing on, I do not mourn that shortness of life. Rather, I take greater value in it because it is so short. Precious moments have a tinge of eternity about them because they are eternally internal to my existence. They go wherever I go, and that is a comforting thought.

Indeed, I revel in knowing that life is bigger than me, that life will continue even after I pass on. There is boundless joy in knowing that the sun will rise and set, that the north and south winds will continue to blow, that will rivers go to the sea, yet never does the sea become full when I am no longer here. I take great comfort in understanding that the world and all its wonders will still be here for my children and grandchildren and even those beyond; why should life be only for me?

The life that God creates is meant to be bigger than any one person, and I take great joy and comfort, knowing that all life will continue to exist after I am gone. Why should existence end just because I passed on? Don't our children, our brothers and sisters, family, and friends deserve a full life? I want life to continue for them and for the countless people born after them, whom I will never know. And if we do indeed have an afterlife, I can't wait to hear their life stories and the marvels and mysteries they beheld that I never did. L'chaim, l'chaim, to life! No matter how long or short it may be.

Ecclesiastes 1:8 goes on to say—"All speech is labored; there is nothing man can say. The eye is not satisfied with seeing nor is the ear filled with hearing."

I agree with this train of thought. We humans talk a lot; we're constantly searching and listening, and much of it is wasted on selfish pursuits. Such is our vanities of vanities as we seek to make ourselves happy and complete through the acquisition of material things and in the indulgence of sensual pleasures. But like Qoheleth implies, we never get there do we? And yet even

Chapter 1

this incompleteness this restlessness is a hidden gift of God because all of that talk, watching, and listening comes with an additional gift: curiosity!

Admit it, you enjoy learning, don't you? I sure do. Well how do you learn? By listening, by watching, by speaking and asking questions, by immersing ourselves in an activity; by our labor! So, yes, our ears are never filled up to total satisfaction that we no longer need to hear anything, our eyes are never so filled that we need not search for new horizons, and we will never stop asking questions or telling marvelous stories of our lives to others while we bear this mortal coil. Our minds do not find final rest because we will never have total knowledge. We are forever seekers, creators, and builders. Thank God for the unfulfilled life!

What a strange thing to say, isn't it? Yet when we are unfulfilled, we seek love, and we explore, build, and create to become fulfilled. Our world is filled with wondrous songs and dances, as well as countless stories of love and courage by unfulfilled people! We have inventions galore, knowledge of things previously unknown, and cures for sicknesses because someone somewhere was not satisfied with what was but wanted something better. In a word they were "unfulfilled." So they spoke and asked questions, they listened and learned from others, they watched and observed in finer detail the world around them. They touched others in love and hate and were transformed because of it, and in the building and creating transformed others.

But, you argue: "Shouldn't our main goal in life be to be fulfilled? Shouldn't we truly know without a doubt our true purpose in this temporary life of ours?" Maybe, and if it is, then you'll never get there by moaning about the temporariness of life, or asking why you exist in the first place or what will happen to you and your works after you are gone. This precious life you have is the biggest classroom and adventure you'll ever have. What you can't do is stop speaking, listening, touching, tasting, smelling, and asking questions that may never have a satisfactory answer. For human fulfillment is often found in the journey and the exploration, not necessarily in reaching a specific goal.

Since this is a spiritual journey for me, all my senses, all my thoughts, all my longings and desires, and efforts whether on purpose or by chance are for communion with the God who created me. My purpose, my personal reason for existence, what I consider my "fulfillment" have transformed over the last seven decades. I have fully accepted my temporariness in this life but do not see my labors of love, whether for my wife, children, grandchildren, church, nation, or God as wasted, whether mankind remembers me or not. For me, at the end of my short life, if all of creation forgets me, I can accept it as long as God remembers me. For if God forgets me, then truly, vanity of vanities, I never existed.

If you want to take encouragement from anything, take encouragement from this: God created you to love you and to be loved by you. He will never, ever forget you if you seek to love Him with your whole being. God created the human soul immortal, not mortal. Your body will disappear like dust in the wind, but your soul will continue into eternity. Eternity, as they say, is a very long time, and eternity's path will wander to many places, times, and realities. For is not heaven a different reality? Our time on that path in this life is but a sentence or a page in that immense book of eternity, but our time here and now will determine many of eternity's paths that we take when we turn the next page of life, when we pass from this one to the next. Speaking of time and eternity Qoheleth (1:9–11) has this to say:

Chapter 1

What has been, what will be; what has been done, that will be done.
Nothing is new under the sun.
Even the thing of which we say, "See, this is new!"
has already existed in the ages that preceded us.
There is no remembrance of the men of old; nor of those to come will there be any remembrance among those who come after them.

My handwritten comment after the saying above was: "But God remembers!" In terms of new things, perhaps the writer is correct, and there is nothing new under the sun. The optimist and joker in me thinks; "What about other suns?" Through the wonders of science, people can now peer into the heavens and wonder if there is anything new under those suns. God, it seems, has made a very big universe that stretches on and on into who knows what end. I often imagine that God has made it so big so He could challenge Himself; and so that under the rules of physics and space and time, birth, death, decay, and rebirth, He may also explore and create new things that never existed until the universe was born by His spoken word. God is said to be the master of time and space, that He is eternal and all knowing. Yet, my imagination wonders if perhaps He created a universe where He purposely set Himself up to not know everything. It is an interesting idea to think of God as a seeker.

Do you think that God ever gets bored with us or this marvelous universe He created? If you know everything from beginning to end, if you can control everything from beginning to end, where is the challenge in creating? Why, as the Ecclesiastes sage asks, do anything if everything was already done, if everything is pre-ordained, and if that which is to come has already existed in ages past?

Perhaps in my ignorance, and I do admit to ignorance on many levels, God created our universe for a twofold reason. First and foremost is to draw all creatures with souls to Him. Second, and this is surely conjecture on my part, to create something so large and so vast that it would challenge Him, much as life challenges us from the day we are born to the day we die. So, how do you draw souls to you? The answer for me has always been through the threefold principle of faith, hope, and love. God has the power and strength to force humans to comply with obedience and fear of God. Fear of the Lord, the ancients said was the basis of true knowledge and wisdom, and the founding structure of religion. Fear is a great motivator for compliance. Fear can help you respect a thing's power to inflict damage. Constant fear unfortunately leads to spiritual burnout. Fear can be used effectively to gain your attention, but only love in its truest and most innocent and pure form will get someone to stay with someone else for the long haul. Only love helps you grow as a person and a creature with a soul that has a direct line to Almighty God, under the right conditions of hope, faith, and love.

So how does an almighty, all-knowing God draw you to Himself in love? What roll-of-the-dice does He throw into the equation of life and existence to get the ball of love rolling?

He does the greatest thing He could ever do. He relinquishes power and foreknowledge (perhaps except in emergencies) and allows free will; for the sake of introducing love into all creatures He has endowed with a soul; for to give up power is to give up foreknowledge of things to come. In an ironic twist of spiritual truth it is by allowing free-will that a destiny of communal love with God is actually possible.

With all of His encompassing power and might and creativity, with all of His all-knowing, none of those powers draw me to Him as much as His all-encompassing love. His love for me makes me to want to worship Him, not fear Him. His love makes me want to entrust my life to Him, to offer Him my prayers, sacrifices, gifts, thoughts, and my very life if need be. If ever I am to be in a complete union of love with and for the God that created me, then for me at least, everything, in every moment of my existence, will be new under the sun. Does a God who created me for such a relationship sound like someone who would forget me, who would blot me out of existence and be remembered by no one?

I think not.

> **(Eccles.—1:13–15)**
> "A thankless task God has appointed for men to be busied about. I have seen all things that are done under the sun, and behold, all is vanity and a chase after wind. What is crooked cannot be made straight, and what is missing cannot be supplied."

In my handwriting under the above comment, in my tattered old bible I wrote: "What about chasing after God?" I wrote that because I partially agreed with the saying that our efforts are a "chase after wind." I've worked for fifty-plus years of my entire life, and some of it didn't have much meaning beyond getting a paycheck to pay for food, clothes, and shelter and some nominal pleasures. However, I have found that my search for a meaningful loving relationship with God had focus and purpose. It had power to transform. It was not meaningless or a vanity of vanities pursuit. How successful I have been or will be is yet to be determined. For me, it has not been a chase after wind to chase after God.

"For in much wisdom there is sorrow, and he who stores up knowledge stores up grief" (v. 18). There is much truth to this statement. Aren't there many things in our lives we wish that perhaps we would have been happier in an ignorant state of bliss? Yet the very wisdom that gives us sorrow or grief (i.e., harsh truths) tells us not having that wisdom would lead to even greater grief and disaster. True wisdom prevents us from repeating Adam and Eve's mistake in the Garden of Eden. Wisdom does indeed come slowly through the slow drippings of life's pains, but the greater truths revealed and properly understood can also lead to right paths and much joy because we do things from love and wisdom (i.e., knowledge properly applied to our lives, at the right times). And as to "much knowledge storing up grief," doesn't it matter which knowledge we seek that either leads to grief or happiness and fulfillment? Whether we wish to openly admit it or not, our minds, our desires, are constantly pulled and drawn to knowledge of good and evil. We've never given up our desire as human beings to eat the fruit of the Tree of the Knowledge of Good and Evil.

So we eat that fruit of the knowledge of good and evil throughout our lives, and our souls pay the price for that knowledge for good or evil.

Chapter 2

Study of Pleasure Seeking:

I said to myself, "Come, now, let me try you with pleasure and the enjoyment of good things."" But behold, this too was vanity. Of laughter I said: "Mad!" and of mirth "What good does this do?" I thought of beguiling my senses with wine, though my mind was concerned with wisdom, and of taking up folly, until I should understand what is best for men to do under the heavens during the limited days of their life. (**2:1–3**)

    I agree with this statement if a person's goal is to find fulfillment and purpose in the pursuit of pleasurable things (i.e., hedonism) or laughter. They are not an end to or a means in-and-of themselves. Yet, for all the despair Qoheleth writes about, near the end of chapter 2, he alights upon a good reason for one's labor, for some pleasure seeking, and for some laughter. He says: There is nothing better for man than to eat and drink and provide himself with good things by his labors. Even this, I realized is from the hand of God. For who can eat or drink apart from him?" (v. 24).

And of mirth in chapter 8, he describes a reason for what I call "honest mirth." The type of honest laughter one has when they see the folly of human ways and their own ways Or of seeing children and lovers struggle to learn how to love properly, not the evil laughter of laughing at the downfall of enemies or of innocent people. He says:

"Therefore I commend mirth, because there is nothing good for man under the sun except eating and drinking and mirth, for this is the accompaniment of his toil during the limited days of the life God gives him under the sun." (v. 15)

Our bodies, our senses, are the vehicles by which we humans learn. There is no learning in this life where there are no functioning senses. Without our senses, we could not even imagine God. Without our senses we could not laugh, love, or labor. Yet, ever do our senses distract us from the greater spiritual realities, or at least their possibilities. Our senses can even distract us enough to the point where we don't even labor for our own self-care (i.e., addiction). Without discipline of the mind, our senses will control us, ever seeking for the next pleasurable activity. Regardless of what catastrophe that pleasure might bring us to.

Verse 15 above hides in plain sight a profound truth about human happiness. We remember and experience many things in life, some pleasurable, some painful, but what memories are the most consistent in the library of contentment and happiness, such as meal memories with family and friends! We work, labor, create, avoid, destroy, come and go in the context of the human family. Is not one of our greatest simple but powerful pleasures in this life the meals we share with family and friends? Aren't our holidays, birthdays, births, and yes, deaths, reasons for gathering together and sharing our life's stories and experiences? Aren't those meals the reason behind some of our fondest memories? So, on contemplation, it seems very true that, as verse 24 says, "There is nothing better for man than to eat and drink and provide himself with good things by his labors. Even this, I realized is from the hand of God."

Qoheleth goes on to discuss the seeming futility of labor if the final fate of the wise and the fool is one and the same: death. Yet, wisdom is given its due for he says: "I went on to the consideration of wisdom, madness and folly as much as light has the advantage over darkness. The wise man has eyes in his head, but the fool walks in darkness. Yet I knew that one lot befalls both of them" (vv. 13–14).

Qoheleth also goes back to the theme that no matter what endeavor a person takes up, no matter how new it seems to him it has been done before, for he says:

> But when I turned to all the works that my hands had wrought, and to the toil at which I had taken with such pains, behold! All was vanity and a chase after wind, with nothing gained under the sun. For what will the man do who is to come after the king? What men have already done! (vv. 11–12)

He also goes back to the idea of being remembered once a person passes on. He says:

> Neither of the wise man nor of the fool will there be an abiding remembrance, for in days to come both will have been forgotten. How is it that the wise man dies as well as the fool! Therefore I loathed life, since for me the work that is done under the sun is evil; for all is vanity and a chase after wind. vv. 16–17

Perhaps my labors, my creations are a vain effort for self-aggrandizement to somehow be known in this world, my feeble effort to be remembered for all time. Yet, I do realize that I and my works will disappear over the ravages of time's unfurling. Any memory of me and my existence will fade into darkness and dies with the last person to remember me. I also realize that I have no control over what I leave behind, whether they are works of art, music, science, or even relationships. People will do with them as they will. They will interpret them as they will and judge me and my conduct and creations according to how they see the world and not necessarily as they really were when the life breath of God was in me. They will do the same to you.

But I do not despair over such bleak thoughts. I did once when I was younger. I wanted to be known, to be famous for something so good that none would ever forget me. Such was my vanity. Yet, knowing that all things in this life eventually go into darkness and dust does not stop my desire to create, to love, and to be loved. If by my existence I give another joy and happiness, if I can ease someone's pain, even but for a moment; if my creations, limited though they be helps someone gain some wisdom or helps them make a closer connection to family and friends or feel better about themselves and especially help them connect closer to God, then I am content, even knowing that those things I do and say are as temporary as the leaves that fall from the trees in autumn. I am content and happy because my existence, no matter how short-lived, mattered to someone else. I made someone else's life better. I had an impact that rippled beyond my own little existence.

So death and darkness will come for us at the time God has appointed it for us. We will not escape it. Yet for all the dread it brings, ever the light of God's love for us burns bright, and even darkness and death will not extinguish it.

Study of the Fruits of Toil—To Others the Profits:

> And I detested all the fruits of my labor under the sun, because I must leave them to a man who is to come after me. And who knows whether he will be a wise man or a fool? Yet he will have control over all the fruits my wise labor under the sun. This also is vanity. For there is a man who has labored with wisdom and knowledge and skill, and to another, who has not labored over it, he must leave his property. This also is vanity and a great misfortune. For what profit comes to a man from all the toil and anxiety of heart with which he has labored under the sun? vv. 18–22

Inheritance is something you leave behind for someone else, willingly or not! My father left his children a small inheritance when he left us to go to the other side of life. He could specify who got what and how much they got, but he had no control over what we did with what he left behind. Such was death's parting gift from the previous living. Whether we spent, invested, or saved any funds, or kept or threw out any belongings or mementos was done according to the receiver's whim, not the givers. So Qoheleth is right; the fruits of our toil do go to another upon our passing, and whether the other person uses those hard-earned gifts wisely or foolishly, the giver has no control or knowledge of how they will be used.

One of the saddest examples of this truth was when I worked for a nursing home in Syracuse, New York, as a security guard back in the 1970s.

One of our jobs as security guards was to bring a deceased nursing home resident's family the resident's final belongings. Time after time, I would witness family members collect jewelry and TVs and then ask us to throw out old mementoes, furniture, and clothing. This made sense since most families already had those things at their own homes. What didn't make sense and was to me the saddest were all the old family photos they asked us to throw out. Remember these people were of the World War I, Depression, and World War II eras. What they didn't realize was that not only were they throwing out valuable family history, they were throwing out history itself!

Countless pictures of mid- and turn-of-the-twentieth-century history went into the trash bin. Photos of old Ford Model T cars and old trucks and tractors, of vacations to exotic and national parks, weddings, baptisms, communions, bar and bat mitzvahs, beloved pets, military and 1920s and 1930s Civilian Conservation Corps (CCC) service photos. Pictures of friends and relatives were relegated to the dust bin of forgotten history. There were pictures of friends and relatives that helped build America and built a prosperous middle-class lifestyle, and helped build the families who were tossing out that family history.

What most of them probably didn't realize was that if they were lucky enough to get old, they would very probably develop a keen interest in their family history, where they came from, why they came, who came and built a new life in America, and how they did so. Years later perhaps in a moment of melancholy when the grim reaper was close to knocking on their doorstep, they suddenly would realize what they lost in those trash bins and wonder if their family and personal history would also be relegated to history's trash bin. That longing for knowledge from whence we came is why I think Ancestory.com has become so popular in the age of the internet.

Yet all is not lost in death and despair. God gives you an awareness of an intangible inheritance that you can leave behind that may even outlast the memory of you. You can leave a bit of yourself in the family and friends you leave behind by teaching them and giving them an example of a life well lived with honesty and integrity. My father, my grandparents, my mom, and my sister and brother who have passed on, as well as my many aunts and uncles, instilled in me the values of hard work and strong family ties. They left me with the understanding of the need for hugs and kisses and a listening ear when you cannot really do anything to alleviate someone's pain and grief. They also taught me the importance of religion, which is a community focused on the love and worship of God and the love of one's neighbor. They instilled in me the love of learning. My father instilled in me the idea of not trying to control the dreams and aspirations of his children. He supported whatever we wanted to do or become.

These are the intangibles of inheritance. They are indeed left to those who remain, and sometimes those left behind don't even realize that some of the things they do and say are because they absorbed the intangible qualities of honesty, integrity, and love you gave them while you were with them. The material things you've left behind, whether willingly or unwillingly, will be spent and used up; they do not last. What will last and have a positive effect over a person's entire lifetime are the characteristics and traits that helped make them the good person they are. You will be remembered not for the things you left behind but because you gave of yourself to others. For you can give no greater gift than yourself, in love, to others.

Those gifts are only possible if you willingly give them the most valuable and precious gift you can give them: your time. When you give another person your time, you are literally giving them a piece of you and of your life. You could be off doing any number of things that bring you pleasure and perhaps even a sense of fulfillment. Your time on earth is precious and is not to be wasted. When you give up your time, you are giving up yourself to another. That time you give others cannot be taken back, so give of yourself and time carefully. When a parent or a spouse, or a friend, and even strangers gives up their time to another, whether or not they realize it, they are in communion with the other person. You are sharing a piece of yourself with another; you are communicating in communion with another person the deeper parts of yourself. In those moments of communion, of sharing, you are inadvertently sending your spiritual essence through and into another into eternity. If the quality of that sharing, communicating, and communion is to last longer than your own existence, it must be born of faith, hope, and love of God and your neighbor.

Finally at the end of chapter 2, Qoheleth latches onto to the wisdom that all of his experiences and contemplation leads him to; that is:

> There is nothing better for man than to eat and drink and provide himself with good things by his labor. Even this, I realized is from the hand of God. For who can eat or drink apart from Him? For to whatever man He sees fit he gives wisdom and knowledge **and joy**; but to the sinner he gives the task of gathering possessions to be given to whatever man God sees fit. This also is vanity and a chase after wind. vv.24–26

It does not seem a vanity or a chase after wind to me. To me, it seems just. It will be just and fruitful if I but trust that God will send it to those who need it most. If I but trust in God that He will do so, then I no longer need to worry what will happen to the things I leave behind, for God will ensure that they fulfill the purpose He has planned for them. To whatever I plant and sow for another person to reap the benefits after me, I simply pray: "Dear Lord, may You place it in the hands of those who need it most, sinner or saint, hard worker or a lazy fool, and may it ultimately do your will to turn all hearts, minds, and souls to you. Amen."

Chapter 3

Man Cannot Hit On the Right Time to Act

This is my favorite chapter of all twelve chapters in Ecclesiastes. Since I've already provided the wording at the beginning of this book, let's dive into why I love this chapter.

If ever the Holy Spirit of God and the blessings of Wisdom personified favored a man in speaking words of wisdom to others, it was the sage who wrote chapter 3, especially lines 1 through 15. As a lector in my church, Christ Our Light, in Loudonville, New York, I have read aloud these famous words to our congregation numerous times over the years. I have picked these words for family funerals and have heard them read at weddings. I've never grown tired of hearing them. For me, they never grow old. Always, as I read them or hear them, they sound new and wonderful to my ears, mind, and soul. How can 299 words speak so strongly to me? Why such a strong stirring of my soul?

The answer, at least for me, is that they speak to the ultimate purpose of wisdom itself. It is a twofold answer as I interpret those words. First, a wise person can see that there is indeed an appointed time for everything, and a time for every affair under the heavens. I see cycles of life and death all about me. There is a season and a reason for the seasons. There is an appointed time for each of them. There is an appointed time and cycle for life and death. From birth to old age, we go through cycles of birth, growth, decay, and finally death. Even mountains, rivers, and seas have their appointed time of birth, growth, decay, and even death, though much longer on the scales of time.

For many people, those times and cycles are simply marvelous aspects of nature and creation, but they do not see God's creative hands in those cycles and times. For them, it is simply something that is, nothing more. Not so for me. All creation, for me, points to a something or someone even greater than creation itself as the ultimate Creator of life as we know it. My wish is for Him to envelop me into Him, and in doing so see with His eyes, His heart, His mind, and His Spirit. Then I would know (Greek: epignosis) the God of my spiritual journey's final gift of manifestation, of communion with Him, the ultimate Creator of all that was, is and will ever be.

All of creation, with its appointed times and cycles, points me to the Creator who made them and set them in their place and time for birth, growth, decay and death, and in some instances rebirth. In rebirth not so much of themselves but of their children, whether human, animal, fish, fowl, or seed. Our progeny follow after us, and bring a piece of us with them as they go through their own life cycle. In them, then, we are reborn.

Science and technology have greatly advanced the human race's knowledge and understanding of our physical world. We are able to do things only dreamed of by the ancients. Yet, the great cycles with their appointed times and places remain. The seasons come and go and humans are born (for the most part) in the usual way and under the usual circumstances. Our bodies come forth from the tiniest of seed and egg then grow, decay, and die. The heavens, seemingly fixed and immutable, have their own cycles and times. Stars, galaxies, and planets are born, grow and develop, decay, and die, though on a time scale that dwarfs even the life cycles of land masses, mountains, rivers, and oceans. Even within cycles that seem like they will last forever, there is an appointed time for change. They stretch and challenge the mind to try and understand them. When understanding and knowledge come, it is only the first fruits of wisdom. Knowledge and comprehension is not the end product of wisdom.

For wisdom to bear its final gift to humanity, to the curious and seeking mind and soul, it must impart the knowledge, and the will how to use that knowledge correctly. Knowing something, how something works, what its cycle of birth, growth, decay and death is, will not give us power or the will to use that knowledge properly. For wisdom to flourish, humans have to properly apply to their lives what to do with the knowledge wisdom gives us. Ultimately we are speaking to right judgment as to what actions we should or should not take within a given situation. If we are wise (Hebrew chokma—Latin—sapientia), we have the unique ability to distinguish what is wise from the foolish (unwise), and we correctly use the combination of knowledge, experience, and a sense of intuitive understanding to make the right decisions in any given situation.

I have always, and still do, struggle with where does the font of will and commitment spring forth from? I have belatedly come to realize that the consistent use of our free will and prolonged sense of commitment comes from what we truly love. There are many things we like, things we'd like to do. If our interest is piqued enough, we may even dabble in those things. However, once we come to realize we don't actually love the things we're doing, will power and commitment slowly and sometimes rapidly fades away.

I like and do love using my oral, artistic, and literary skills, but they in themselves were never enough to make a fully conscious free will commitment to develop them at their highest level of excellence. So over seventy years, I would dabble in them but never stayed with them long enough to develop those skills to a higher level until, after many years of reflection (with the help of my journals), I came to realize that despite my many imperfections I truly loved God and my relationship with Him. He has become my "Precious," with apologies to J.R.R. Tolkien. It was that realization that fired up my free will and commitment. Thus was born this very book that made it to completion and even unto eight edits before submitting it to publishers.

Find your true love, and you find your will to commit to something with your whole being.

Lines 1–8 speak to "a time to . . ." It is the wise person who can understand those times to properly act or to withdraw from a given situation. It is the wiser person who does so. For me, it has been and continues to be a lifelong lesson. The class for obtaining and using wisdom properly is still in session!

The Problem of Retribution:

"And still under the sun in the judgement place I saw wickedness, and in the seat of justice iniquity. **And I said to myself, both the just and the wicked God will judge, since there is a time for every affair and on every work a judgement.**" vv. 16–17. I think if we live long enough, all of us get to see injustice allowed by the very institutions that are supposed to prevent injustice. American history, let alone world history, is replete with the powers-that-be meting out an unjust sentence upon the innocent for the sake of retaining their power. Even very young children have a sense of injustice. Thus the proverbial saying "taking candy from a baby" shows the injustice of the act by the angry tears of the child so unjustly denied. Sadly, in this life, on occasion, evil wins, at least in the short term. The innocent are sometimes punished unjustly and are not vindicated in their lifetime. They must rely on God's final judgment for the vindication and justice they seek.

Where I have seen God's vindication in those instances is in the simple passing of time. The evil men do cannot be hidden from Him forever. What is wrought in darkness is brought into the glaring light of truth through the passage of time and an emotional removal from the issue by those who came after the injustice and could see with clear eyes the injustice of an act.

I see it in America constantly. From the way Native Americans were mistreated, to the evils of slavery, to the oppression of the worker, or the destruction of the environment, no evil deed goes unnoticed by the eyes of time and history. In the short term, it seems that God allows it. Some say that is justice delayed and thus justice denied. However, God seems to take a longer view of injustice. I have noticed that wrongs are often righted when the evil deeds of people are piled so high that society cannot ignore them. As painful as it is, a just society deals with the sins of their fathers and their own sins. Dealing honestly with the past causes turmoil, grief, anxiety, doubt and a whole host of negative emotions, thoughts, and feelings, we'd all rather not deal with if we're honest. But God has put into our hearts the need to right a wrong, to set history straight, and to correct and eliminate the wrongs of the past and present. From my observation, it is never a smooth process.

If I may digress a bit, it seems to me that America is in a constant state of addressing the wrongs of the past and present not properly dealt with in their own time. That is not a bad thing. If anything, it speaks to a people whose spirit is being constantly stirred by the Almighty to right a past or current wrong, to acknowledge it and to provide a remedy for those still experiencing the same injustices. America, even from its founding was never perfect. America may never be "perfect," whatever that actually means. America, however, has never given up on striving to become a more perfect union by:

> We the People of the United States, In Order to form a more perfect Union, establish justice, insure domestic Tranquility, provide for the common defense, promote the general Welfare, and secure the blessings of Liberty to ourselves and our Posterity, do ordain and establish this Constitution for the United States of America.

I'm not sure America has ever been tranquil; it may never be. That may not be such a bad thing as long as the cause for turmoil and strife is because we are constantly seeking that more perfect union through true justice for all and not just for some privileged few. While we draw life's breath we must continue the pursuit of justice in our own time so that future generations will not have to correct our mistakes; so God will not have to either. We may lose that fight on occasion in this life, but God will ensure that ultimately we will win the war against injustice in all its forms so that: "Love and truth will meet, justice and peace will kiss. Truth will spring from the earth; justice will look down from heaven" **Psalm 85:11–12.**

May I offer a prayer for all of us? Lord, grant me not a vindictive heart, rather help me to rely on You for vindication and justice served, even though

I be in the right. For righteous anger can quickly turn to wrath and hatred, and hatred into evil, and evil to the destruction of my soul. Please do not deny me justice in this life, but if it is to be denied or delayed, create in me the courage to accept that my vindication and justice may only come after I am gone. Yet, my hope is ever in Your love for me, and I know that I will indeed see the day of justice and vindication that may be denied me in this life. Amen.

Finally, the last sentence of chapter 3, verse 22, says: "And I saw that there is nothing better for a man to rejoice in his work, for this is his lot. **Who will let him see what is to come after him?"**

At the end of this last sentence, I wrote in my Bible: "God?!." I ended with a question mark, an exclamation point, and a period. The part of me that is like Qoheleth asks the question: who will indeed let me see what will come after me? The part of me that trusts in God to reveal what is to come after me if needed exalts in faith and hope, thus the exclamation point. The part of me that says God's Word is true and to be trusted makes it a statement of spiritual fact, thus the declarative period.

I believe that God in his infinite wisdom lets us have a sense of what might come after us as a form of consolation but not the actual future. I believe there's an excellent reason why we are not allowed to see what comes after us. If we see a destiny that is to follow us, it has the potential to disrupt the future and deny those in the future their free will. If those who came after you knew exactly what their future held, would they even try and change it? Could they even change it at all?

People's destinies may be known by God, but people are kept ignorant of theirs so that whatever decisions they make are freely made. It is no little irony that our ignorance may plant the seeds of the search for knowledge and wisdom and in doing so create a destiny that is filled with purpose. The proper application of wisdom helps make those good decisions. From those decisions, their destiny is fulfilled. Very few of us are given a destiny in the womb before we ever see the light of day. Those that do are usually called prophets. The unusual thing that people don't realize about prophets is that any future they speak about is a direct result of the decisions made by people living in the prophet's own time. Prophets are God's canary in the coal mine of a person's soul and in society's soul, at the time they are told to prophesize.

When I was a young man in my twenties, I was deep into astrology for a while. I was fascinated by the idea that our futures/destinies could be discerned by the movement of stars and planets. I read up on books of astrology and bought astrology books that purported to tell me what my future was going to be. Sometimes they were right. That was the hook that kept me delving into astrology longer than most people. Somewhere along the line, I slowly became aware of a very important truth. Astrology was starting to dictate my decision-making process. What was I supposed to do on Monday; what was going to happen to me on Saturday? Would I face danger this month? Would I see riches come my way? I was slowly losing my own free will for the mistakenly perceived idea of prosperity, security, and safety through knowledge of my future. No more rolling of the dice of life, just follow the day's advice and I'd be set to go!

Something else was happening that I didn't expect or see at first. A certain amount of joy was disappearing from my life because I had stopped to a certain extent making spontaneous decisions. I came to the final conclusion that I'd rather have a life made free by my own decisions and not some star chart that was sometimes right and often wrong. Making free-will decisions doesn't mean I'll know what is to happen right in front of me, let alone what will come after me; and that's fine by me. Life was much more of an adventure and an exploration after I made that decision.

If the good Lord gives you the gift of a long life, you will be able to look back at the previous stages of your life see your destiny up to the point you're looking back. Your earlier destiny is now set in stone; it wasn't back when you were living it. Each moment given to you back then was an open book, a path to be taken or not taken. Time, people, and experience influenced your decision-making process, but you made the decision, no one else.

Now, turn your head from the past to the present and look around you, and if you can, peer into a presumed future with all that it implies for your future health, wealth, and well-being. You have decisions to make: important decisions and not-so-important ones. Each will have its effect and will carve out the rest of your life's destiny. As you travel whatever life you have left before you, remember to take Wisdom with you, for she will be your most valuable companion who will teach you what it is you are actually seeing and experiencing, and most importantly, what you should be doing in and with those experiences.

Chapter 4

Vanity of Toil:

"**Again I considered** all the oppressions that take place under the sun: the tears of the victims with none to comfort them! From the hand of their oppressors comes violence, and there is none to comfort them!" 4:1. There is indeed in this world of ours oppressors and the oppressed. Often there is no one to comfort them. Since we can see the truth of this statement, what is our role under the sun that God has given to us when we see people unfairly oppressed with no one apparently able to comfort them or to free them from their oppressors? I believe we inherently, and spiritually, know the answer to those questions. We are charged with the work God has assigned us to, that within our own abilities and means, we are to comfort the oppressed and, if able, free them from their oppressors. It is not vanity of vanities to do so. Even if our words and actions do not bear immediate fruit of freedom or comfort, it cannot be an excuse to not try.

    For some of us, the pain and suffering we observe is so close to home that we must become directly involved. We risk life, limb, and reputation to right the great wrong that stands before us. Others more removed from the violence and sufferings are no less called to do something for the sake of justice and peace. We are not all called to directly take up sword and shield in defense of the oppressed and suffering. However, we are all called to do something to assist those unjustly oppressed. Even those far removed from such things cannot turn their heads, lower their eyes, and mumble, "Well, it's not in my backyard, so it is of no concern to me." God calls all of us to action when faced with injustice and suffering.

Before the emergence of the digital world and media, the world might be forgiven if everyone everywhere did not immediately jump at every act of injustice, oppression, and suffering. Distance is no longer a reason or an excuse to not act rightly. Today we are too connected to avoid seeing the oppression and suffering that occurs all over the world. A person cannot turn on the radio, TV, or our cell phones without seeing someone, somewhere, being oppressed and suffering unjustly. God calls all of us to do something to right the wrong, to free the oppressed, and comfort the suffering. Even atheists, agnostics, and humanists know that we must help each other in times of trouble. How much more so are we who call ourselves children and servants of God to act?

Yet, we know we cannot end all oppression and suffering. Sometimes the scale of it all intimidates us into inaction. With fearful heart and trembling lips, we ask: "What can little ole' me do to end all of that evil?" If we are honest with ourselves and with God, we're just making excuses to not act in His holy name. I'm going to use a very strong word here for what we become when we do nothing in face of assisting someone who is facing unjust adversity and it is within our ability to do so: cowards.

Time after time both in the Old Testament and in the New Testament, the Lord admonishes us to not do evil. The Word instructs us time and again to avoid evil (that would cause us to sin) in all its forms. God never tells us to let evil be, to not confront it. He also tells us when we do confront evil, we will not do so alone if we ask Him for His help when we do so.

There are many ways and many levels we can confront oppression and suffering without risking life and limb. In America, it seems that donating funds to worthy causes is the main way Americans fight suffering and oppression. Those funds do help to end oppression and comfort the suffering. With tongue firmly in cheek, to paraphrase a Bible quote: "Of charities, there is no end!" We can and do volunteer our time and effort. We can confront oppression verbally, not only as individuals, but with entire groups of people united for a single cause. We can write our leaders to take action; we can and do protest. We can and do change and eliminate laws and regulations that oppress and hinder equal access to resources or even cause us to break the law because the law itself is unjust. On the personal front, we can promote the cause of justice and peace by individually promoting the cause of love of family, friend, neighbor (immediate and worldwide), and with God's special grace, love of our enemies (that last one I know I can't do without God's grace).

Do not fool yourself into thinking because you are young or old, rich or poor, small or large in stature, male or female, or even, Lord forbid, be oppressed yourself that you can exempt yourself from the need to confront oppression and comfort the suffering. The Bible makes it abundantly clear that while life has its saints and sinners, the person God detests the most is the person who does nothing to lift a finger to help their fellow human being in their hour of need. They will not be able to stand before God in final judgment and say they did no evil. They cannot say because they didn't steal or lie or murder or cheat or covet their neighbor's spouse or goods that they deserve entry into His heavenly kingdom. The sin they did commit was that they did nothing when something had to be done to confront evil, to free the oppressed, and comfort the sufferer.

So yes, Qoheleth is right; there is oppression that goes unpunished and suffering that goes unheeded. Let it not become vanity of vanities on our watch. In whatever way we can, small or large, and always, always, with God's love and Spirit, let not the final story of oppression and suffering be that they won, but that they lost because we fought the good fight and that oppression and suffering did not have free reign, but was defeated because the people of God, filled with His Holy Spirit, would not let it be so.

"And those now dead, I declared more fortunate in death than are the living to be still alive. And better off than both is the yet unborn, who has not seen the wicked work that is done under the sun" vv. 2–3. There is no denying that there is wicked work that is done under the sun. Since the fall of Adam, evil has had its way with this world in ways unimaginable and horrifying. The counterpunch to evil has always been humanity's recourse to the Lord for protection, guidance, and wisdom in order to either avoid evil altogether or to defeat it. We are also called to avoid and, as necessary, fight evil in all its forms so that the wicked work done under the sun can never reach its full force or potential. We seem really good at going to God during a time of crisis. There's an old saying in the military: "There are no atheists in foxholes."

What is the most effective strategy to fight evil? We know that evil grows in the dark places of our minds and hearts. Evil is a parasite. It is a soul-destroying virus that needs good, not evil, to grow. Evil feeding on evil only leads it to a quicker death. Evil is not happy with a quick death. It wants to prolong its existence through the suffering, corruption, and destruction of the good. While evil's ultimate future is its own self-destruction and death, it is not happy until it takes the good down into corruption and decay with it.

The most effective strategy for destroying evil is to bring it to the light of day and truth. The most effective light of day and truth is to be found in the heart of God. Under God's light, love, and truth, evil shrivels up into nothingness and naught, but love remains.

It hurts to bring evil to the light of truth; especially when it is our own evil that needs to be brought to the light of God's truth. There are essentially two ways that evil is brought to the light so that it might be obliterated. The first is to use our free will to admit our own evil, to see it for what it is, and what it is doing to us and those we love. That is the first step to healing. That first step sometimes can only come about with the assistance and grace of God. Admitting sin and powerlessness to fight it is a hard pill to swallow. Yet, and I speak from personal experience, only if we ask God directly for that help and grace will we ever have a chance at defeating the evil within us.

The second way that evil is brought to the light of truth is God's way, devoid of human desire or experience. For the sake of those He loves, He wrestles evil with His omnipotent love and holds it up to His light of love and truth. In His hands, in His light no evil can escape. Under His omnipresent gaze, evil withers and dies. My prayer for all of us trapped in evil's icy death grip is that we have the humility and strength of will to ask for God's grace and assistance in cleansing us of any evil we might secretly harbor, rather than forcing God to hold our evil up to His truth and light against our will. Death and life He sets before us; let us choose wisely least He chooses; against our will, for us. Amen.

Let us dive into the subject of prosperity. What we don't do often enough and well enough is to keep God's presence with us in times of prosperity. At least in terms of faith in the Almighty, it often appears that when the going gets good, the good seem to forget God. It's not always the case that we forget God in the good times. I've noticed as I've gotten older, older people do not forget the author of their good times. Older people do thank God for the good times because with death getting ever so closer to them, they have learned just how precious those good times are.

As usual, I digress! So, is it better to have never been born? Is it better to now be dead if we were once alive? If it was better never to have been born, or having been born to now be dead, it would seem life then is a curse. Life itself would be seen as evil. Nonexistence or death over life would be seen as a blessing. Why would a loving God do such a thing? The answer is He doesn't.

All of us, even atheists, instinctively know and understand that life is a blessing and not a curse. It is human beings that make a life's work evil under the sun. God doesn't, and neither does life. If life is evil, then we have only ourselves to blame. In the old newspaper comic strip "Pogo," written and drawn by Walt Kelly, Pogo said: "We have met the enemy, and he is us!" Life can be and sometimes is hard, but it is not evil.

Even if you have had a hard life, and for many people, life is hard, there is no sugar-coating hard times when they happen. Would you be happy with the alternative—death? Most probably would not. If I might use a bit of gallows humor here for a better perspective on life and death, often when I talk to very old people, they are often suffering from a host of health problems. Aches and pains seem to be married to old age. When I ask them how they are doing, many of them say the following: "It's better than the alternative!" They are affirming the desire for life over death, even with all the pain they are experiencing. The other funny thing older people say is: "Well I check the obituaries every day, and if I'm not in it, I figure I'm doing OK!"

Another type of gallows humor comes from people I've met over the years who've survived a major illness or accident. They sometimes say: "Well at least I'm not looking up at the grass just yet!" What they mean is that they're not in their coffin, looking up to the grass above. They've survived and are grateful they did. My own personal gallows phrase goes something like this when someone asks me how I'm doing: "Well I'm walking and talking, and I still have my marbles, so I guess I'm doing OK." You may notice my desire for a quality-of-life old age. I hope it stays that way until my last breath, but I understand that it may not be so.

The antidote to such dark thoughts that death or nonexistence is better than life or the living is to re-affirm the beauty of life itself. We need to remember the sweet and good times in our lives so that they can give us the strength to persevere through the hard times, and get back to good times.

So, Do You Remember:

> The first time you felt cool grass between your toes and the feel of sand on your hands as you made a sand castle on the beach? Do you remember splashing in puddles on a rainy day or the joy of your first pet?
> Do you remember the feel of soft fur, the sound of a purring cat or kitten, or the many licks of a new puppy? Do you remember your mother and father's warm embraces? Can you remember lifting your face up to the sun with your eyes closed, feeling the warmth and maybe a cool breeze playing with your hair? Do you remember the smell and beauty of flowers, and sight of tall majestic trees and lofty mountains?

Chapter 4

Can you remember your first lover's kiss and embrace? Do you recall the pounding and beating of a young heart in love for the first time? Can you remember the joy in the newness of things or of learning something for the first time? Can you remember the joy of meeting and making new friends for the first time? Can you remember all the playtimes you had with those friends? And, yes, can you remember the sweet pangs of a broken heart that made you think you'd just die, but you didn't? In fact, you went on to find a new love just as exhilarating and wonderful as the first, perhaps even more so since you now knew you could lose love if you did not care for it tenderly. Your loss made you feel and value new love even more than when you first fell in love. Do you remember holding your firstborn in your arms for the very first time? Do you remember your child's first steps or words spoken? Can you remember sending them off to kindergarten for the very first time? As a grandparent, can you remember piggyback rides and Ring-Around-the-Rosy and grandchildren opening their Christmas or birthday presents from you and seeing the delight in their eyes and the joy in their excited voices?

Can you remember your first job and first paycheck and the feeling of independence it gave you? Can you remember the teenage rite of passage of learning how to drive a car for the first time and getting your driver's license; an official recognition that you were on the road to full adulthood and independence from your parents? Do you remember the feelings of accomplishment as you graduated high school and/or college? Does your heart and mind stir with passion at the sound of music, or the hearing and/or watching of a good story? I don't think that normally you would forget your wedding day or the birth of your children. Let us not forget parties and holidays, and good meals shared with family and friends.

The list of life's affirming experiences could go on and on, but the main point is to ask: "Having experienced some or all of those things, including the hard times that life gives us, would you really trade them for nonexistence or even death"? Would they have been a blessing by not allowing you to experience those things? I hope not for both our sakes.

For Believers in God in Support of Your Hope, Faith, and Love:

Do you remember when you first felt His presence, that, deep inside you there resided "Another," guiding you, loving you, teaching you, and drawing you ever so closer to Him over time and life's experiences? Do you recall the stirring of your soul in amazement and wonder of His holy and living Word, as revealed through the scriptures? They weren't just stories to you, were they? They touched you in a place you didn't even know existed.

Do you remember your first prayer answered and the joy it brought? Did you ponder deeply when the answer to your prayer was "No"? Did you look at the wonders of nature and see a "Creator's hand" and not just the law of physics, biology, of weights and measures?

Have you ever been lucky enough to experience the "consolation of the Holy Spirit"? Within that consolation and presence of the Holy Spirit, were you overwhelmed with an immense sense of peace and love and a spiritual communion with the Creator? Did it make you feel as if you never wanted it to leave, that you could just rest there forever and be eternally happy?

Did you feel the stirring and the warning of your soul and the diminishing of the presence of God's Holy Spirit when you willingly decided to follow your own desires that lead to hurt and abandonment?

Do you see the face of God in the face of others? Do you see the presence of the Holy Spirit in others as they went about the good works of God here on earth? Do you feel the joy and presence of the Holy Spirit when two or three of you gather in His name?

There is a depth to God that science will never comprehend but that the soul through hope, faith, and love may come to know, for it is the only way He will ever let you know Him during our earthly sojourn.

God bless believers one and all. Amen

Continuing Qoheleth's thoughts:

"Then I saw that all toil and skillful work is the rivalry of one man for another. This also is vanity and a chase after wind" vv. 4. Competition, rivalry, the desire to dominate, to be the best, to be number one, to be a G.O.A.T. (Greatest of All Time) impel the drive to be remembered for all time. There's no denying the truth of that statement. Capitalism wouldn't exist without it. Dictators, kings and queens, emperors, and Caesars seem to thrive on that idea. Wars have been fought because of it. It truly seems like a vanity and a chase after wind. Americans seem to be brought up with that philosophy in tow. Perhaps the whole world is. Still, God makes nothing evil in and of itself. Even toil, skillful work, and rivalry of one man against another have a place in the world. The world progresses on many fronts because of competition and rivalry. It is especially true in the areas of science and technology. Many medicines and machines that have proven useful in upping the standard of living for people were the direct result of competition.

Humans want to be skillful; they want to be very good at something and known for being very good at something. I know I do and pretty much always have. Our earliest competition and rivalry came by those closest to us: our brother and sisters. Whether we "fought" for Mom and Dad's attention, or to be recognized as better than our siblings (Ex. "Who do you love more

Mom/Dad?), it was rivalry and competition. As children, how many of us can remember either trying to be better at some things that our brother or sister did, or altogether learning something new and be very good at it that our brother or sister wasn't?

A funny thing happens as you get older and hopefully wiser. We begin to understand that always trying to be number one is a chase after wind because there's someone always out there, who sooner or later will be better than us at what we do. God forbid if what we do becomes irrelevant to society. In terms of career and self-identity, there's almost nothing worse than understanding that what you do is obsolete.

If you're lucky, the direction of the spirit of competition changes—and changes for the better. You decide (or realize) that the person you're really most in competition in with is yourself. That's not a bad thing if you apply the proper attitude to competing with yourself. You realize that learning and becoming a better version of yourself and of what you've chosen to do with your life doesn't end at graduation or receiving a certificate of graduation or completion. Life is your never-ending school of exploration and adventure! That's not a bad way to turn competition and rivalry on its head for a good purpose: the betterment of yourself.

There are some great benefits to this way of thinking. You don't worry so much about what someone else is doing, or if they're better than you. You are even able to learn from them without that bugaboo, jealousy, which tends to cloud one's mind and thinking. You're actually able to enjoy life more for what it is, rather than for what it can give you or advance you. If you're lucky enough and you are able to find like-minded individuals, your joy of learning and the number of accomplishments you obtain increase exponentially because of and with the people who've joined you on your journey of learning and exploration.

You will also find old age a lot more fun! I worked in a nursing home organization for almost eleven years in Syracuse, New York. Old folks can teach young folk a lot about how to live life and enjoy it. I always noticed the happiest older people were the ones who (1) kept a sense of humor, (2) kept on learning new things, (3) enjoyed socializing, and (4) had a hobby or focus that they carried in to old age. I saw older people with good health who were miserable in old age and seemed to be waiting to just die. Then I would see older people in bad health but had the attitudes described above and they were happy! They laughed much, sang, socialized, did arts and crafts, and physical exercise at the level they could do. We mourned their passing because a little light went out in the world when they left us. Yet, they did leave some of their light behind in the memories and attitude toward life that had their effect, and they affected, in a positive way, those of us left behind. So in closing, go ahead and compete against yourself; you'll always end up in first place!

Companions and Successors

> Again I found this vanity under the sun: a solitary man with no companion; with neither son nor brother. Yet there is no end to all his toil, and riches do not satisfy his greed. : For whom do I toil and deprive myself of good things?" This also is vanity and a worthless task. Two are better than one; they get a good wage for their labor. If one falls, the other will lift up his companion. **Woe to the solitary man!** For if he should fall he has no one to lift him up. So also, if two sleep together, they keep each other warm. How can one alone keep warm? Where a lone man may be overcome, two together can resist. A three-ply cord is not easily broken. vv. 7–12

These passages seemed to abound with common sense. Most of us were born into a family of some sort. We are meant to be a social, community people. There may be some jobs, some tasks that a solitary person can complete (ex. writing), but most work is done with other people. Blessed is the person who finds a true friend and companion who shares a common task. And, even more blessed are companions who share a life's journey with each other.

Common folk wisdom throughout the ages, across all races, cultures and times, point to the need for working with other people on a common goal. All of them warn of the dangers of going-it-alone. The "fall" is hard indeed when you fall alone. I believe it is a blessing from God that we are born first into a family, then a broader community, and as adults, join a community of fellow workers. Our very identity, our sense of self-worth, even to an extent, our sense of reality is intimately wrapped up in the relationships we build over our lifetimes.

Common folktales across time, all races, and cultures also speaks to the lonely miser, alone with his/her riches yet never happy. There is no amount of accumulated wealth that makes them happy or feel secure. In terms of Western culture, perhaps the best-known tale of the solitary rich man alone with his money, yet never happy is Charles Dicken's "A Christmas Carol." Yet he does find redemption in coming to understanding the true meaning of Christmas and ends up finding he is much happier spreading his wealth around and socializing with old friends and family members. In a mixture of Western and Eastern culture the Greek myth of King Midas and his golden touch resonates among all cultures about the dangers of always wanting more and more. Even the food he touched turned to gold until he wasted away from starvation, surrounded by his wealth, which as Ecclesiastes dutifully notes: our wealth upon our death ends up going to another; vanity of vanities indeed!

Americans across our own history have been sold the myth of "Do it yourself," "Pull yourself up by your bootstraps," "Rugged individualism," and "God helps those who help themselves," which; by the way, God never actually said in the Bible. Even the military falls into that insidious trap with a recruiting phrase of: "An Army of One." I served thirteen years in the US Marine Corps and US Marine Corps Reserve. Show me a one-man army or a one-man Marine Corps doing battle, and I'll show you one dead U.S. Army solider and one dead US Marine. A more apt phrase as hinted by Ecclesiastes is: "United we stand, alone we fall."

Ecclesiastes 4:11 also says: "So also, if two sleep together, they keep each other warm. How can one alone keep warm?" I suppose if you pile up enough blankets a person could keep warm, but sleeping alone isn't for me anymore. After forty-six years of marriage to my wife Peg, the best body warmer a man could ever have, I'll skip the extra blankets! Nuff said!

> Better is a poor but wise youth than an old but foolish king who no longer knows caution; for from a prison house one comes forth to rule, since even in his royalty he was poor at birth. Then I saw all those who are to live and move about under the sun with the heir apparent who will succeed to his place. There is no end to all these people, to all over whom he takes precedence; yet the later generations will not applaud him. This also is vanity and a chase after wind. vv. 13–16

My Bible interprets the first sentence as the king issuing forth from his mother's womb, and even though of royalty, is brought forth naked and poor, bringing nothing into creation but themselves. One is reminded of the oft-said phrase: "You come into this world with nothing and you leave with nothing." You can be buried with great fanfare and in the grandest of mausoleums, be buried with all your wealth and the finest clothes, yet, you will still take nothing with you on the other side of life.

When I was a young man, I used to fantasize about being buried under some magnificent monument that would be visiting by countless people over the years to come and pay their respects to this "great man of powerful and everlasting good and great deeds." God and life humbled me pretty quickly on that fantasy! I'm glad He did too! It was a dumb idea. What really made me realize the futility and silliness of such an idea has been visiting the cemeteries of all the family and friends I've lost over seven decades of life. The stones get old and dirty, grass cracks the stones and grows in between the cracks, and moss covers their names and dates of birth and death. Each year Peg and I, as well as Peg's sister, Mary Louise, plant flowers in their memory. We try and clean the stones, and say prayers over and for the dead. We do remember and revere them. For us, they are still very much alive in our memories and in the character traits we adopted from them, seeing in them the good fruits those characteristics brought them. Yet time inexorably marches on, and decay will win the day and the night. There is no stopping it. Time will not even relegate us to the dustbin of history. Time will relegate our physical presence and even the memory of us to dust in the wind; where we will land will not be known. So I will "cast my bread upon the waters" and let the river of life take the memory of me and my acts, both virtuous and evil, my creations, my words written and spoken, my loves and hates out to the seas and oceans of a physical and spiritual universe that only God could have imagined, and trust that wherever it lands is where God meant to plant that essence of me.

And as noted above others will take our place, and others will place their allegiance to those left behind after we are gone. Why should I complain about that? If I owe an allegiance to a dead person, it's to keep their memory alive if they were a good person and to remember not to repeat the acts and words of evil people. Life is for the living, not the dead. Worrying whether or not people will still be loyal to you and follow you even into death won't make it happen. If you must bring your allegiance to anyone, bring it to God. He never dies, His truths remain from generation to generation, His love for you will never die, and He will never, ever forget you.

I have to be bluntly honest here. I would still like to be remembered forever by, at least, the people I loved and whom loved me. I would like for time and decay not to erase the memory of me here in this life. Yet, even that idea I'll give up as long as I'm remembered by God because if He remembers me, then so will all the other wonderful souls I've loved in this life. That hope, that love, will only happen as an act of faith here in this life in order for it to become my reality in the next life.

Vanity of Many Words

"Guard your step when you go to the house of God. Let your approach be obedience, rather than the fools' offering of sacrifice; for they know not how to keep from doing evil" v. 17. Whether you attend religious services in a temple, mosque, or church or some other sacred place, I hope you go with reverence and fear of the Lord, that you go not because you feel obligated to go, or you "have to go," but because you've come to recognize His presence in your life and that over time, you've come to recognize His many blessings that gave you good times, good family and friends, and meaning in life. I hope you go because even in hard times, and perhaps especially in hard times, you recognized His spirit of consolation and guidance that got you through or is getting you through them now. And most importantly, you attend because you truly worship Him with all your heart, mind, and soul because you feel deeply His love for you, and you want to return that love through proper-minded religious worship in fellowship with brothers and sisters wrapped up in the Holy Spirit of love.

There is a very important phrase above which states: "Let your approach be **obedience**; rather than a fool's offering of sacrifice." Obedience is a tough word for all of us born of human flesh. The heart wants what it wants; the human will shall do as it wants, obedience be damned! I believe that the phrase is pointing out that it is more important to follow and act in obedience to our faith, hope, and love of God and our neighbor than in merely following religious rituals and practices. Religious rituals are given to us for our spiritual benefit, but they hold no meaning or significance for us if, after performing those rituals and offering up those sacrifices, we return to thoughts and actions that are contrary to God's will for us, which is to love God with our whole heart, mind, and soul and to love our neighbor as ourselves.

Lip service to God (i.e., praising and sacrificing to Him but doing evil instead of good) is unacceptable. Such people are known for what they truly are: hypocrites. The just reward they are expecting because they complied with religious rituals and sacraments will not be the one God will give them in the final judgment.

Chapter 5

Be not hasty in your utterance and not let your heart be quick to make a promise in God's presence. God is in heaven and you are on earth; therefore let your words be few. For nightmares come with many cares, and a fool's utterance with many words. When you make a vow to God, delay not its fulfillment. For God has no pleasure in fools; fulfill what you have vowed. You had better not make a vow than make it and not fulfill it. Let not your utterances make you guilty, and say not before his representative, "It was a mistake," lest God be angered by such words and destroy the works of your hands. Rather, fear God! (5:1–6)

The example for the word vow in the dictionary says to make a vow is to solemnly promise (pledge, commit) to do a specific thing (ex. an act, service, or condition). Its older definition is to dedicate someone or something, especially to a deity. Many of us when we were younger might have made a vow/promise to God if He did so-and-so and/or such-and-such a thing for us, we would do something specific in return. I have heard from people in dire straits that if God would only heal them or save them, they would dedicate themselves to do something in honor of being saved. A woman I once worked with had a serious illness. She told me she asked the saint whose middle name she had, that if she would intercede for her for a cure she would thereafter go by her first and middle name. Then when asked why the change in name, she would explain how she was cured of the serious illness through the intercession of her namesake saint. She fulfilled her vow.

Another woman I knew had a close relative go to war, and she promised God that if that person came home safe, they would never eat chocolate again. That person did come home safely, and she did indeed fulfill her vow and never again ate chocolate.

I, too, made promises to God when I was younger. I almost never had to fulfill the promise because for reasons only known to Him, the answer back was no; He wasn't going to do what I asked! Ouch! No's are tough! My Christian faith has made me leery of vows to God or, in fact, to anyone. That doesn't mean no vows should ever be made. I made my wedding vows over forty-six years ago and so far, so good! When Peg and I sign a contract, whether it's for a car or home or appliance or for a service, it is a form of a vow. I haven't, to the best of my recollection, broken any of those vows either. As I've gotten older and hopefully a little wiser, my vows have become few and far between. The words Jesus spoke so long ago about making vows to God have really sunk into my belief system. He says:

> You have heard that it was said to the people long ago, "Do not break your oath, but keep the oaths you have made to the Lord!" But I tell you, **Do not swear at all**: either by heaven, for it is God's throne; or by earth, for it is his footstool; or by Jerusalem, for it is the city of the Great King. And do not swear by your head, for you cannot make even one hair white or black. Simply let your "Yes" be "Yes" and your "No" mean "No." Anything more is from the evil one. Matt. 5:33–37

This passage has come to mean to me that my word is my bond. If I can't keep my word, swearing to God or heaven won't make it happen. In fact, not only will God be angry with us, but so too anyone we make a promise or vow to that we do not keep. There are a few other reasons I am afraid to make a vow to God. First is my own sinfulness. If I, who proclaim my love and fidelity to God can't keep from sinning, how can I even have the presumption that I am even capable of fulfilling a vow? As I've gotten older, I've learned to control my mouth much better than in my youth. Too often my mouth was working before my brain became engaged, often to my own detriment!

Another reason is learning from people who are always asking you to promise them something but don't keep their own promises or won't commit to a similar promise. Those people are the "users" of life and other people, and I've come to the conclusion that I will not give pigs my pearls (e.g., my promise). I have often found that such people, even when they won't promise, tend not to even keep their own word. They appear to be without integrity. They are not "whole" persons. Knowing that sometimes circumstances don't allow us to keep our word (ex. imminent danger), I now often preclude giving my word to someone to do something by saying: "If it is God's will, I will do it." I found more often than not that when I gave my word to do something for God or a fellow human being, if I tried to do it within what I see as God's will for me, I often succeeded in my efforts.

Finally, one of my main reasons for not making a vow or promise in God's name is that I do indeed fear Him. I dread His punishment, but I absolutely loathe the idea that I would break my vow to Him. To break my vow to God is to willingly separate myself from His presence in my life. How can I betray such love as He has given me? I know that I am capable of such a thing, but His presence and His love for me so overwhelms me that as I slowly mature in my hope, love, and faith of Him, the chances of being so spiritually stupid diminish with each passing God-loved filled day. Still, I must remain on guard against my own spiritual foolishness.

So, is there a vow we can make that is acceptable to God and one which we can give our all to keep? I think there is, and it's a pretty simple one. If there is one vow to make in our lifetimes and to keep, and from which, simply giving your word will be sufficient, instead of having to vow to do something. It is what God has asked of us from the very beginning of our creation.

We can vow to love the Lord God with all our might, with all our heart, mind, and soul, and to love our neighbor as ourselves.

It seems to me if we fulfill that vow all other things we give our word to do will succeed, and in ways unimagined except in the heart and mind of God.

Gain and Loss of Goods:

The covetous man is never satisfied with money, and the lover of wealth reaps no fruit from it; so this too is vanity. Where there are great riches, there are also many to devour them. Of what use are they to the owner except to feast his eyes upon? Sleep is sweet to the laboring man, whether he eats little or much, but the rich man's abundance allows him no sleep. vv. 9–11

Chapter 5

Whom do you covet; whom do you worship; whom do you adore; whom do you love?

I have met the covetous man, and he is me! If there is a human being alive who doesn't covet something deep within the bosom of their heart, I haven't met them yet. For some people, the thing they covet (their god!) is indeed wealth; for others, it's material possessions; and for some, it's possession of another human being, or for power and influence. If we covet, if we desire something at an unnaturally high level to the exclusion of other good things and people in our lives; we have become slaves and worshippers of the things we covet. I say slaves in every sense of the word. Slave because the thing you covet to the exclusion of all else now owns you. You may think you are pursuing and possessing it, but long ago, it trapped you in its icy death grip. You have become like Gollum in The Lord of the Rings, in love with your "Precious" to the exclusion of all other things in life.

As Ecclesiastes points out, you probably don't sleep well because you're too worried about losing the object of your desire. There always seems to be someone "out there" who wants what you have. And it's true, if you do possess the thing you desire, what can you do with it, except look at it, maybe fondle it now and then? It does nothing for anyone, not even you. The fear of losing the thing you coveted diminishes the joy you would have by possessing it. Even if you have the strength to give up this thing you covet, you are not free of its insidious grip if you can't free yourself from the very idea of coveting something. If you are free from one possession simply means you'll move on to another coveted obsession.

Happy the person who is content in their labor, who enjoys the fruit of their own labor, who can take pride in the work of their hands and mind, and who does not covet their neighbor's goods.

In a paradox of spiritual covetness, if you must covet something or someone, covet God! Hold Him close to your heart, mind, and soul. Hold Him ever so tight. Look on Him longingly and lovingly. Let your soul swim in the vastness of His eternal love. And if you would go even deeper into His Spirit, give Him away! Share Him and the Good News with others so they, too, can "covet" God. The more you share God in faith, hope, and love with others, the deeper will go your individual and community relationship with Him, until you no longer covet God. You will just simply abandon yourself in Him and His eternal and infinite Spirit of love. In abandoning yourself, and immersing yourself in Him, with Him, and for Him in the unity of the Holy Spirit, and in letting God possess and covet you, surprise!, everything your soul ever truly desired will be given to you, for everything belongs to God, and it is His to give freely to those who love Him. Amen.

> Here is what I recognize as good: it is well for a man to eat and drink and enjoy all the fruits of his labor under the sun during the limited days of the life which God gives him; for this is his lot. Any man to whom God gives riches and property, and grants power to partake of them, so that he receives his lot, and finds joy in the fruits of his toil, **has a gift from God.** For he will hardly dwell on the shortness of his life, because God lets him busy himself with the joy of his heart. 5:17–19

So ends Chapter 5 on a positive note. It is indeed a good thing for a person to eat and drink and enjoy the fruits of their labor under the sun. There's an old saying about work that rings true throughout our lives. It goes something like: "If you do not enjoy the work you do, you have a job. If you do enjoy the work you do, you have a career." Another saying is: "If you love what you do, you'll never work a day in your life!" In the early chapters I expounded on the joys of meals with family and friends and how, despite the many work and career memories we have, we seem to remember and cherish those friends and family member meals the most. We look forward to them especially during the holidays if we're lucky enough to be able to join with friends and family for a feast. In regard to work, if you are able to enjoy the work itself and if lucky enough, the end product that your works gives you, then you are triply blest.

The fruits of our labor vary with the type of career we're engaged in. The language used in Ecclesiastes often evokes the imagery of an agricultural society, which it often was back in those days. Today, with the advancement of technology and science, the fruit of our labor varies greatly. If you are a farmer, you indeed do have fruits (and vegetables!) of your labor to enjoy. If you are a musician or in the performing or visual arts, you have something tangible to enjoy, whether it be playing a piece of music, or performing in front of an audience, writing a song, or completing a drawing, painting, or sculpture. If you are a chef or cook, you not only get to partake of the fruits of your labor, so do a lot of other people, which in turn increases your joy in the work you do.

Others of us may have a career with not-so-solid or physical returns. Teachers who are able to impart knowledge in their students enjoy the fruit of their students' success and realize that their "personal fruit of labor" is to be able to successfully teach something to others. People in the medical fields, whether physical or mental, enjoy the fruit of their labor when they help a person recover from and accident or illness, or at least minimize the pain their patients are enduring.

If you are or were a bureaucrat in a civic or government position (as I and my wife were) the fruit of your labor is in getting needed goods, services, and resources to the people and organizations that need them to survive and even thrive. It may sound silly to some people, but I took pleasure in finishing a well-written report on time, or reviewing and approving an application for government funds to an educational institution that needed the information in the report or the funds that were generated by a successfully reviewed and approved application.

Those whose career is in the spiritual field, the fruits of your labor are less visible. Healing a broken spirit or a broken heart, and helping people to draw closer to God is not always discernable to the eyes. It needs to be a lifelong commitment and passion of yours if you are ever to be successful. Success will be measured mostly at the individual soul level, and you may never see the fruit of your labor. What a blessing it is when you are able to see someone healed from a broken heart and spirit because of your labors, your blood, sweat, and tears. If, through your efforts, you are successful at helping people to connect to God at a deeper level, your place in heaven is especially blest.

Life gives us big jobs and little jobs. It gives us tedious jobs, monotonous jobs, fun jobs, jobs that can be done quickly, and some that take a lifetime to complete—and some that we know we'll never complete but must be worked on for the good of others. We're extremely lucky if we can take joy in all of them. Some of the most menial and boring jobs physically can be emotionally and spiritually satisfying. Fellow parishioners often comment to me, as we're busy folding church bulletins, stuffing envelopes, and sealing them, how it's actually enjoyable because it creates a chance to talk and socialize with friends, and the work itself can give a sense of normalcy in life and a sense of stability.

We call them "chores" because they don't take a lot of effort and have to be repeated day-after-day. We can sometimes catch ourselves sighing heavily as we contemplate another day of endless chores. Yet, as the years roll on, the "chore" of completing a daily task takes on a different meaning. We may complain about them and mildly begrudge having to do them over and over, but we come to realize that they actually can give us a sense of being alive, that we're not looking up at the grass from down below!

Another word for it might be routine. Yes, we can get stuck in a routine, and too much routine can be dangerous to our mental health if we don't go outside that routine on occasion in order to give ourselves a chance to learn new things and to grow spiritually, mentally, and emotionally. However, on the positive side of things, that routine can give us a sense of our place in life and lend a sense of stability to our lives. Our sun comes up and goes down, the moon comes out along with the stars, another day awaits us, we're still here, and we've things to do an accomplish, so let us then make the most of the large and little things that will come our way today, and may God show us how to enjoy the things we still can do.

So whether you've just successfully completed a brain operation, completed a painting, played some wonderful music, sang an emotionally moving song, if you've just finished a report on time, or cleaned your house, finished making your bed, or stuffed envelopes for your place of worship, accept that gift from God, and dwell not too heavily on the shortness of life because God lets you busy yourself with the joy of your heart. May it ever be so, Lord. Amen.

Chapter 6

Limited Worth of Enjoyment:

> There is another evil which I have seen under the sun, and it weighs heavily upon man: there is the man whom God gives riches and property and honor, so he lacks none of all the things he craves; yet God does not grant him power to partake of them, but a stranger devours them. This is vanity and a dire plague. Should a man have a hundred children and live many years, no matter to what great age, still if he has not the full benefit of his goods, or if he is deprived of burial, of this man I proclaim that the child born dead is more fortunate than he. 6:1–3

Qoheleth's main point is that if a man toils all his life and he is unable to reap the benefits of his efforts, the child born dead is better off than the man because the child will never know the anguish of working for nothing. Qoheleth goes on to say in verse 6: "Should he live twice a thousand years and not enjoy his goods, do not both go to the same place?" If we put it on an emotional level, it is the home built but never lived in, the engaged person who never marries, the pregnant woman who never gives birth, the college degree earned but career in it never found, the crop planted and harvested but never eaten or sold for profit, it is the successful work of a lifetime stolen by another. It is the pension earned but never partaken of because death came too soon. We reasonably expect that in life our efforts will be rewarded, that we will enjoy the fruits of our labor. When the fruit of our labor is denied us, whether by chance, choice, accident, disease, or violence, it crushes our soul. There is no avoiding or denying the pain that it brings to us.

In our multi-media society of twenty-four-hour news feeds there is no denying that this type of tragedy happens. Are there any potential solutions to such a sad ending? Perhaps.

In being denied the fruits of our labor, we need to contemplate God's gift of wisdom on the proper use of materials things. The word balance once again comes to mind. Work is a gift of God and the materials and benefits made possible by our labors are also gifts. Gifts will do us no good if we "don't open the package" to see what's inside and to make use of the gift given to us. Wisdom tells us that a balance must be struck between partaking of the fruits of our labors and preserving the fruits of our labors for a rainy day that may or may never come.

Do you work hard? Have you accumulated some material wealth? Have you had a chance to enjoy the fruit of your labors, or are you hoarding those fruits? Do you use those fruits to manipulate others into doing your will? Despite all that you have, do you harbor the feeling that you need still more in order to feel safe and secure? From what, lawyers, disease, accident, vengeful ex-lovers? If what you've accumulated doesn't actually make you happy or feel safe and secure from the impending (or imagined) apocalypse, why then do you need more of the same?

So the solution, to an extent, is spelled out back in Ecclesiastes 2:24; "There is nothing better for a man than to eat and drink and provide himself with good things by his labors. Even this, I realized, is a gift of God." Putting the previous verse simply, make sure you indulge yourself a little, once in a while, of the fruits of your labor. Waiting for a far-off, unforeseen date where it will finally be safe to enjoy all the fruits of one's labors may never come. How many lives have we seen over the years cut short through no fault of the person who died? The rich and powerful, the important, the poor, and those with little or no influence can and do all die at unforeseen times.

God's wisdom teaches us that the opposite philosophy of life is just as wrong as hoarding one's material fruits for some unforeseen future date when all those fruits of labor will now be needed or safe to use. That is the idea of "Eat, drink, and be merry, for tomorrow we die." Saving for a rainy day isn't just folksy wisdom; it's prudent to do so. Prudence with one's wealth is a virtue. It doesn't mean to never enjoy the benefits of your labor but to use them wisely. To use your material benefits wisely doesn't mean to use them only on yourself. There was once a famous rich man who once said: "Money is like fertilizer. If you spread it around, it will help grow things, if you just let it sit there it raises a stink to high heaven. And heaven, my friends, doesn't like the smell!"

Another final point to make is one Ecclesiastes seems fixated on: leaving one's wealth behind and not knowing what will become of it. The somewhat simple solution to that problem is the use of the spiritual gift of charity. Giving some of your material wealth away while you still draw breath gives you some control over how it will be used. Even very rich people who are not necessarily spiritual by nature know this simple truth. My prayer for you is that the gifts of your labor, freely given, for reasons of love, precede you to your heavenly entrance and final judgment so that they may stand in good stead as to the character of your soul before God and the entire heavenly host. And whether you kneel or stand before the Lord, may the wisdom of the Holy Spirit grant you the insight that your lifetime of labors, of charity and love, and the sum total of all your life experiences has made you the divine fruit of God's labors. Amen.

"What the eyes see is better than what the desires wander after. This also is vanity and a chase after wind" v. 9. The footnote in my Bible says that this statement means that the good that is present to us is better than that which is absent, and perhaps unattainable. It's hard to argue with this statement. It boils down to the old adage; "A bird in the hand is worth two in the bush!" It's funny in the odd sense that we humans never seem to be quite happy with what we have. I'm not sure if we're brought up by society and culture to see that wanting more is a good thing, or if we're just born with that innate desire to grab for what is always beyond our reach. If someone is happy and contented with what God and life has given them, we pass judgment on them and call them lazy. We deem progress more important than being content with the basics of life. Having more is seen as a sign of success; being content with what one has is seen by many as having limited vision and desire.

I know I struggle with being content with the basics of life. I still like to buy things I don't need. I like to accumulate things that catch my eye. I like to partake of the "better things of life." I not only look to see if the grass is greener on the other side, I want to know if there is even any grass on the other side! I'm not a rich man by any measure of the meaning of the words, yet my hutches are full of things I've picked up over the years as well as things from deceased relatives. I've never needed them, but I do like them.

I will say the advancing of the years has certainly dampened the urge to acquire and accumulate. Heck, I'm running out of space to put anything! Yet God's wisdom once again shines through the aging process that we are all prisoners to. The closer to death's door I get, the less I care about accumulating wealth or things except as an inheritance for our children. I realize that the things that are important to me most probably won't be important to my children. Those things hold memories of experiences important to me, not to them. If they do not illicit an important memory and emotion to them, then they'll end up in the trash or to someone who can actually make use of them.

As usual, I digress from the main point of Qoheleth's statement. My prayer on that front is simply may all of us learn through the wisdom and grace of God to appreciate and cherish the gifts He sets before us, and not worry or be saddened by gifts we were never meant to have. Amen.

> Whatever is, was long ago given its name, and the nature of man++ is known, and that he cannot contend in judgement with **one** (one=God) who is stronger than he. For though there are many sayings that multiply vanity, what profit is there for a man? For who knows what is good for a man in life, the limited days of his vain life (which God has made like a shadow)? Because—who is there to tell a man what will come after him under the sun? vv. 10–12

I often wonder, was I given my name long ago before I was ever born? Was my life on this plane of existence then a destiny or a free-will offering? Why do I so strongly, even in the midst of my many imperfections, feel so drawn to Him? Why do I feel the need to be with Him, in Him, in the unity of the Holy Spirit, forever, and ever?

I see other wonderfully religious and spiritual people who seem to be able to rest ever so gently with His spirit. I do not rest gently in His Spirit. My spirit is restless for Him and in Him, even when I am enveloped in His Spirit. I twist and turn, I grasp and seek, I cry and laugh almost at the same time, I swim and fly and drown in His spirit. I even try and run away from His spirit when it seems I will lose my entire being in Him. I am no longer Leon, but someone, something else, entirely. I become fearful of Him. He's too much for me. Yet, ever He draws my soul back to Him.

Whatever my name was, was given long ago, and the nature of me was not known, even to me, unless He revealed myself in Himself, in me. God is too strong for me, even when I fruitlessly try and contend with His Spirit moving within me, changing me, overwhelming me, and overpowering me with His love. I surrender and rebel, surrender and rebel, each time surrendering more and more and rebelling less and less. My spirit is overwhelmed with a love and a presence I cannot comprehend, or grasp, or ever fully understand. I cannot add or detract from His love. I can only accept or reject; nothing more. So I accept His love and am forever changed and transformed into a new being, an alien to my old self but never more fully my real self because He resides in me, and in my own small way I in Him.

Question: "For who knows what is good for a man in life, the limited days of his vain life (which God has made like a shadow)? Because—who is there to tell a man what will come after him under the sun?" 6:12

Answer: God's love and presence is good for a man in the limited days of his life, and it is God who will and does tell him what will come after him under the sun, for all paths under all the suns in the universe lead to Him. My prayer for us is that whatever paths we take, whether separately or together, may we all end up at the same destination: in the loving arms of God Himself. Amen.

Chapter 7

Critique of Sages on the Day of Adversity:

> A good name is better than good ointment, and the day of death than the day of birth. It is better to go to the house of mourning than the house of feasting, for that is the end of every man, and the living should take it to heart. Sorrow is better than laughter, because when the face is sad the heart grows wiser. The heart of the wise is the house of mourning, but the heart of fools is the house of mirth. 7:1–4

THERE IS A counter-intuitive wisdom to some of the sayings above. I don't think many of us would disagree that a good name is better than a good ointment. My Bible footnote says that this phrase simply means that ointment applied to a child at birth has its effect only for a little while; however, a good name remains even after death.

There are few things in my life that can arouse my indignation and righteous anger. Someone disparaging my good name which I have taken a lifetime to build is one of those things that can make me very angry. On most fronts in our short lives, a good name will hold us in good stead when seeking justice. That's because a good name is earned and not given. A good name is earned through hard work, honesty, and the loving and caring for and of others. A person with a good reputation (i.e., good name) is seen as a person of integrity, a "whole" person. Their relationships, their business dealings will more often than not bear good fruit (i.e., success).

I have personally seen that a good name does indeed follow a person even after they have passed away. There are many relatives and friends, who because of the good people they were, are fondly remembered by those left behind. More than once in my life has someone shared with me a personal story of how a friend or relative passed on to them gems of wisdom that they've used in their lives and that they're still using to this day. Rarely is a person with a bad name, a bad reputation, listened to while they are alive or dead. It's hard to trust a person with a bad reputation, even when they are speaking a truth. My prayer for all of us is that we see a good name as more valuable than silver and gold, or found treasure. May we develop that good name for ourselves as if it were a living breathing thing; which it is because it's attached to us. Amen.

Let us now move on to the counter-intuitive portion of Qoheleth's statement. Most of us do not naturally gravitate to a house of mourning. We naturally gravitate to a house of feasting and mirth simply because they make us feel better emotionally and physically. On a personal level, I really gravitate to a house of mirth. For me, laughter is the best medicine against the onslaught of life's slings and arrows of outrageous fortune (Thank you again, William Shakespeare). Yet I instinctively know that too much mirth and feasting isn't good for me (my Buddha belly tells me so!). They distract me, lead me astray, as it were from the more important tasks at hand that I've been avoiding simply because they are painful to deal with.

There is another wise man who speaks like Qoheleth who is not in the Bible but understands the importance of learning from our pain in order to gain wisdom about the really important things in life. His name (and good reputation that follows him even unto today) was the Greek philosopher Aeschylus and he wrote the following: "He who learns must suffer. Even in our sleep, pain which cannot forget falls drop by drop upon the heart until, in our own despair, against our will, comes wisdom through the awful grace of God."

Pain and pleasure are both teachers of humankind. Pleasure teaches us to want to stay where we are (in the pleasure). Pain, if interpreted correctly, teaches us the how, where, why, and when of an experience. If our desires can be overcome, pain can lead us to the wisdom of understanding our folly and provide the means (i.e., knowledge and wisdom) to either avoid the pain, overcome the pain, or get though the pain. You may have noticed that I wrote: "If our desires can be overcome." Have you ever witnessed in life people, perhaps even yourself, who will put up with almost unbearable pain in order to obtain the object of their desire? We humans have a rather odd and unique ability to turn a blind eye to the pain that wisdom is using to try and teach us that something isn't good for us.

We misinterpret the pain and sometimes even death as a mere obstacle to be overcome in order to obtain that which we desire. Or we see pain, oddly enough, as a motivator to continue our quest for that which we desire. We have a wonderful capacity to constantly and consistently misinterpret what God and life is trying to teach us, because "the heart wants what it wants." My prayer for all of us then is that may our hearts always want God before all else because all else that we want will flow from the love of God, and our heart will receive not only what it wants, but also what it needs. Amen.

The third part of Qoheleth's statement speaks to the house of mourning and that sorrow is better than laughter when seeking the gift of wisdom. Death and mourning are indeed bringers of wisdom if you are willing to accept their gifts, painful as they may be.

There is another element to the gaining of wisdom that Qoheleth does not mention enough in my opinion. That element is the passage of time itself. Add up the passing of the years with times of mourning, sorrow, and tears because of the passing of loved ones, and you begin to see the preciousness of life and how fleeting it is. You truly begin to see the importance of the people you love in your life. You start to obtain a reverence for life and the people you love. The older you get the better you are able to discern (Aha—wisdom!) what is really important in life. Things become less important, and people and our relationships of love with and for them start to take first place in our lives. We are even able to examine more clearly what actually makes us happy, and we are then able to alter our behaviors and desires to go for the better things in life that make us truly happy.

So Qoheleth is correct; death, sorrow, tears, and loss can teach us wisdom if we are willing to accept their gifts. Willingness is the hard part. I have to be ruthlessly honest here. I hate pain! I hate learning anything through pain. If I can, I avoid pain at all costs. Pain is a teacher and class I'd just as soon as not be a student of. Yet wisdom teaches me that if we are born of flesh and blood, we cannot avoid pain and the lessons it does and can provide if we are willing to learn from the experience. So my prayer for us is: Dear Lord in heaven, help us to be willing to learn correctly and accept the gifts wisdom can provide us through the heavy experiences of death, mourning, tears, sorrow and loss. Amen.

P.S. I think I'm doing pretty well on wisdom's teachings on the feasting and mirth front. Maybe a little too well!

"This also is vanity, for oppression can make a fool of a wise man, and a bribe corrupts the heart" 7:7. Oppression in all its forms makes a fool of just about everyone because it puts us into our survival mode. Our emotional, spiritual, and intellectual defenses rise up sharply under the whip of oppression. Our sense of injustice explodes forth into a river of indignation and anger. In our anger, if the oppression is too heavy and prolonged, it can easily turn into hate; a blind raging hatred capable of not only destroying the oppressor but also those around us as we struggle to remove the yoke of oppression. In our search for justice and freedom from our oppression, we may inadvertently destroy ourselves in the process.

That is not to say that we should meekly accept our oppression. Unjust oppression in all its forms, whether blatant or subtle, must be fought. It must be fought with all that we have at our disposal. What are most important are our responses to oppression. Whether it is oppression of others that we observe or our own oppression, it is important to seek the wisdom of God on how best to resist our oppressors.

Just as chapter 3 speaks to a time for every reason under the sun; even doubly so the right reason during times of oppression. Sometimes the sword, spear, and shield must be wielded. Other times stealth is required. Sometimes our only option is to escape oppression because we do not have the means to defeat it. Sometimes it even makes sense to be the victim so as to shake the sense of justice from outside sources who can exert pressure that you as a victim cannot. That is the hardest role of all to accept when confronting the evil of oppression. We are not naturally inclined to be a victim—it hurts too much. It makes us feel powerless and weak. Yet, oftentimes in history, when God enters the fight, unbeknownst to the oppressor, God makes the victim the leader and redeemer of justice just as He had His Son do on the cross and at the resurrection. An unbiased look at the struggles of African Americans during the 1960s–1970s and even today shows the power of offering up one's very self for the sake of freedom and justice. The blood of the martyr, the backs of the beaten, the beards plucked, the face slapped unjustly, and the anger not returned is more powerful than any blows inflicted by the oppressor.

Yet for many, and here I speak for myself, I cannot play victim without God's Holy Spirit giving me the strength, will, and protection to do so. I was an active duty US Marine for thirteen years: three years served in the regular Corps and ten years in the Reserves. My first inclination at oppression is to immediately strike back. It's kind of infused in the DNA of my personality, my identity. I have slowly learned that there are some things I cannot do but with the grace of God. It is wisdom and a good dose of humility to know when those times are that we can only do something with the grace and assistance of God. My prayer for all of us is to have the wisdom to know when we need to run to God, not walk, for the gift of wisdom and grace which will instruct us on the best way for us as individuals and as a faith community to break the yoke of oppression, and see the dawn of justice and freedom. Amen.

Let's move on to how bribes can and do corrupt the heart. I don't think we need a long discourse on the statement: "and a bribe corrupts the heart." As much as I am loathe to admit it, I can be tempted to accept a bribe, especially if the bribe is something I actually want. Money and power aren't my weak spot for bribes. I can flick them off like swatting an annoying fly. Things of innocence, beauty, and grace are another story altogether. They do tempt me. I cannot recall actually falling to the temptation of a specific bribe, but God has made me take a hard look at myself; and I know that I have to be careful of such a bribe, especially when wrapped up in the deceiving cloak of a "good thing." Satan knows how to corrupt a good soul by hiding a bad thing that's wrapped in the illusion of a good thing. We end up convincing ourselves that the end justifies the means when deep in our souls we know it doesn't. Suffice to say, know your temptations so you can resist them, for your temptations surely know you, and they will corrupt you when given even half a chance.

"Better is the end of speech than the beginning; better is the **patient spirit** than the lofty spirit. Do not in spirit become quickly discontented, for discontent lodges in the bosom of a fool" 7:8. We do like to talk, don't we? We want to talk and be listened to, and then we want to talk some more and be listened to again. Yet God's wisdom teaches us that of the two, the wise listener is wiser than the wise speaker. The wise listener surveys what is being said and what is happening around them. When the wise listener does speak, he/she has taken into account what the other person has said. The wise listener for the most part does not disparage the other person's statements, even when he/she believes they are wrong. If he/she disagrees, they do not shout over the other person, but neither do they stay silent unless they are in the presence of a fool who only speaks and never listens. Ignorant swine do not know or will not appreciate the worth of pearls before them.

Once many years ago, one of my supervisors and I were having a conversation, and I was getting pretty animated (i.e., loud and defensive), and when I stopped for a breath, he quietly said something to the tune of: "The volume of your discourse will not make it any righter than my quiet opinion." Oops! The boy was put in his proper place. I had a slice of humble pie that day! But I learned something that day, and it stayed with me ever since it was first spoken. I would like to proclaim that I've been a quiet speaker and a deep listener ever since. Nope, no such luck. A passionate view or belief on something seems to naturally turn up the volume on my vocal chords now and then. Still, his words did have an effect because I have been able to quiet my voice more than I used to, and I have been making a sincere effort to be a good, deep listener. His words have helped me to do that over the years.

I also think that what Qoheleth was also trying to say about the end of speech being better than its beginning is because once words are finished, the mind can now engage in thoughtful contemplation of what was said. Thoughtful contemplation allows for a chance at empathy with the speaker or at least sympathy. It also allows a person to consider a new idea or way of viewing things, or to confirm the rightness of the traditional way of doing things. A few moments of silence can give you the appearance of being wise. There is an old saying and I apologize to whoever said it because I can't give credit to him/her, and it goes something like: "It is better to be silent and appear wise, than to speak and be shown the fool." I don't know about you, but I've done both in life and I prefer the former to the later.

Let's move on to the patient spirit being better than the lofty spirit. I was mildly annoyed with that statement, but I do understand the value of a patient spirit over a lofty spirit. I enjoy contemplating and meditating on God, God's nature, and His all-embracing love for all creation. I love being wrapped up in prayer and private conversations with God. Sometimes I receive the gift of consolation and seem to get lost in His embrace. I would happily stay there forever if He'd let me, but He doesn't.

There's a real, physical world out there that needs attending to, and God has given me, in fact, has given each of us a role to play in healing, forgiving, creating, and loving Him and our neighbors and being good stewards of this wonderful planet we call Earth. Those efforts take a patient spirit, not a lofty spirit. Patience is a virtue they say (who are "they" anyway?!). Unfortunately, it is a virtue that we must develop over the entire course of our lifetime. I'm still working on that virtue! It may not seem like it on the surface but waiting, and waiting with the proper attitude, is hard. It is very hard. We're happier doing something, working toward some ultimate result or end game.

Waiting for a response from God sometimes and perhaps most times, requires patience. God will not be rushed, no matter how much His children pester Him for His spiritual cookies. Personally, my two greatest areas where spiritual patience is needed and where I experience spiritual discontent and which I struggle in are in developing and maintaining good social and personal relationships, and in the area of physical suffering. I hate experiencing pain and seeing others I love in pain. If ever there was an area that I am in an eternal struggle of faith, it is in the pain we experience in this life. Sometimes, for me personally, it is only God's grace which allows my faith to survive and perhaps even flourish in the midst of great pain.

Developing and maintaining good personal relationships, including our spiritual relationship with God, takes time and energy. It takes God's grace to strengthen and support our efforts in those areas. And God's grace isn't, nor has ever been a rush job to "get it done." It takes good listeners not just good speakers disbursing imagined pearls of wisdom to others to savor and relish. It takes hard work on everyone's part to develop strong, loving relationships with other human beings and with God.

The other area I struggle with is in areas of prayers for others who are sick or dying and whom I love and care deeply about, and whom I believe are worthy of God's healing power. God is a mystery when it comes to which prayers He answers in this area. I believe in the power of prayer. I believe that when two or three of us come together in His name, He listens and answers the prayer. Yet if His answer is no or I sense no answer at all when I pray for someone I love who is sick or dying, I have a crisis of faith. The patient spirit struggles to stay with me. The lofty spirit is perplexed, and the mind seeks desperately for a way out or at least understanding.

The patient spirit accepts the "No," but the hopeful spirit does not. The lofty spirit asks: "Why not"? The mind and heart struggles to understand and accept. Sometimes the hands of the mind throw themselves up in the air in exasperation and resign to the fact that it will not understand God's "No." The heart and soul tearfully embrace in sorrow. Consolation for those deeply mourning does not seem near or even possible. Yet God's wisdom in His "No" for healing or rescuing, which surpasses human understanding, persists. Often His wisdom is not revealed until the passage of time when the patient spirit comes to understanding. Other times because of the greatness of our sorrow we do not come to understanding until we see Him on the other side of life.

My prayer for all of us who receive "No" for an answer for a prayer on the behalf of someone we love and whom we deem to be a good person worthy of God's healing is: Blessed are those who can humbly accept God's "No," which, in the fullness of time and His loving wisdom, will become "Yes." At that time, the patient spirit is rewarded with the true meaning and understanding of how God's "No" helped each of us to receive from God a "Yes, enter my heavenly kingdom and reside with me and those whom you loved, who proceeded you into my heavenly kingdom, for all eternity." Amen.

> Do not say: How is it that former times were better than these? For it is not in wisdom that you ask about this. Wisdom and an inheritance are good, and an advantage to those who see the sun. For the protection of wisdom is as the protection of money; and the advantage of knowledge is that wisdom preserves the life of its owner. 7:10–12

It's time for some old fashioned dry humor on the folly of human behavior. Have you ever noticed how, if we're lucky, we do indeed talk about "the good old days" and how with the passage of time they somehow seem to get better and better than they were? Sometimes our past life seems to take on mythical proportions. Yet, if we took a truly critical eye at our past, it might not look so rosy after all. There is also another type of person stuck in the past that I've observed over the passage of time. The "Woe is me! Oh, how terrible my life was!" person. They can't get past the real and imagined hurts, and because of that, sours their present and destroys any potential for a happy future. They can't even say the opposite of Ecclesiastes; "How so much more wonderful these present times are than my past times."

When you ask people if they'd want to go back to those times, almost to a person they say no. And I don't know about you, but being a teenager once was more than enough for me! I'll take my present, thank you, and try to make it as pleasurable and happy as I can. There is one interesting thing about going back to the past that many of us have articulated. That is, we would like to go back to our youth, or at least our youthful vigor, but with the wisdom and knowledge we've gained over a lifetime. We would correct our mistakes and ensure as few regrets as possible. We've come to value the gaining of wisdom over a lifetime of experiences and relationships. Most importantly, we do not want to lose the valuable lessons life and wisdom has taught us. The patient spirit is indeed rewarded over the passage of time with hard-fought and earned wisdom. Those tears and laughter, our sorrows and losses, our victories and loves, great and small became the tools and lesson plans of wisdom. If we learned those lessons well, we reap the benefit of a wonderful present and hopefully a happy old age.

Let us speak to the good that comes with an inheritance and the gaining of right knowledge that helps protect our hard earned wisdom, which is like the protection of money (to assist with our earthly needs). When I was almost sixty years old, my father passed away and left a small inheritance to be shared with me, my three children, my younger brother, his son, and my older brother's daughter. My older brother Gary had passed away from prostate cancer when he was only forty-three years old back in 1994. My sister Diane had passed away in 2008 from a major heart attack at the age of sixty-one.

Because my dad did not have Medicaid, only Medicare, the nursing home, because of federal regulations, had to deplete my father's savings until it was two-thirds gone before the federal government would step in to assist with nursing home care costs from Medicaid. It didn't leave much to distribute, but each and every one of us appreciated that our dad/grandfather was able to leave something behind for us. It helped to pay loans and college bills, and house repair bills. There wasn't much, but it did what he intended it to do for us; it eased our financial burdens. Wisdom does teach us to save for that rainy day, and many a family has appreciated inheritance from a parent's that helped buy a house, pay for college tuition, or even helped toward a comfortable retirement.

We can easily see that the protection of our money, our assets, can and does serve a useful purpose as an inheritance or for assisting us with our own current needs. It is wisdom to know so and to do so. So, as Qoheleth points out, do you grow in wisdom and reap the benefits of wisdom? Have you come to even understand what the assets of obtaining God's wisdom are? Do you understand that wisdom leads to a fulfilled life, that it brings us joy, health, hopefully long life, material wealth that fits our needs and wants, and promotes personal and social peace and prosperity? Do you understand that God's true wisdom will help you develop good judgment about the people and things and experiences in your life? Have you come to realize that if you have been developing wisdom as a gift of God that you are listened to, and you can and do influence people? Do you understand that the gaining of right knowledge is not wisdom, but the application of that right knowledge in your life is true wisdom?

My prayer for all of us is that we protect our spiritual wisdom even more than we protect our material wealth. Our material wealth comes and goes, but may God's spiritual wisdom last forever and go with you in the next life and have its positive effects in this life even after you are gone. Amen.

"Consider the work of God. Who can make straight what He has made crooked? On a good day enjoy good things, and on an evil day consider: both the one and the other God has made, so that man cannot find fault with Him in anything" v. 13. I cannot help but consider the work of God. At every sunrise and sunset, at the birth of a baby, the flowering of young love, the aging and perfection of a mature love, nature in all its glory, at my relationships with my wife, children, grandchildren, my friends and neighbors, my church community, even something as ordinary and commonplace as weddings and funerals, I cannot help but consider the works of God. I cannot but help see the hand and heart of God in all these things. To me, all of creation sings of His reality, it dances to His mighty voice, and all creation plays sweet, profound, and deeply nuanced music from the atomic level out to the stars and galaxies and perhaps beyond even our own known universe. And that reality and that awesome Creator and His love reside deep within my soul. Consider the works of God indeed.

Critique of Sages on Justice and Wickedness:

> I have seen all manner of things in my vain days: a just man perishing in his justice, and a wicked one surviving in his

wickedness. Be not just to excess, and be not over-wise, least you be ruined. Be not wicked to excess, and be not foolish. Why should you die before your time? It is good to hold on to this rule, and to not let that one go; but he who fears God will win through at all events. 7:15–18

Let's back up a little bit to the last sentence prior to this section: "so that man cannot find fault with Him in anything." If people ever find fault with God, it is in the first sentence above where it states: "I have seen all manner of things in my vain days: a just man perishing in his justice, and a wicked one surviving in his wickedness." What people forget is that most true evil is from God's gift of free will. It is people who freely choose to do evil, to have a just man perish in his justice—not God. A person either comes to God and God's ways freely or not at all. God has never forced anyone to believe in Him or to love Him, or forced anyone to follow in His ways. God does not usually, directly, correct an injustice. Rather, He calls to those who love Him and have heeded His call and follow His ways to seek to right the wrong, and to the best of their ability to not allow a just person to perish in injustice. When good people choose to do so, when they choose to become the face and voice of God, then I have recognized an energized God who becomes actively involved with those seeking to right a wrong or to prevent a wrong.

The most common strategy I have seen God use in my lifetime is what I call "the miracle of placement." Have you ever had a trying time in life that just seemed so unfair, and you cried out to God for protection, vindication, or healing, and lo and behold, at a time and place you did not envision, the right person showed up to assist you, or the right materials, or the right information was presented to you so you could be protected, vindicated, or healed? Notice that I did not write that God took up your cause personally, but rather, through the presence of His Holy Spirit residing in the ones He loves and who love Him, He stirs up their spirits to come to your aid. His Spirit can and does influence those who do not believe in Him to come to your aid even though they do not realize He is sending them to you in your hour of need. He deftly uses the everyday people, places, knowledge, and materials to come to your aid. God does not hog all the glory of being a hero. Rather, He bestows that privilege on all of us who heed His call to action. We are all called to be heroes for God and His ways.

Something that many people don't realize about God's interactions with humanity is that He is actually a team player! He wants to work with us! He does not want to do everything Himself, even though He has the capacity to do so. Yes, He wants us to only worship Him as the one true God. He wants us to faithfully follow His ways of justice and peace. He wants us to love Him with a faith-filled, fierce love, just as He loves us. However, once those perimeters of faith and love are met, it's game on! Whether He acts as coach or a team player is up to Him, but to participate, and to participate actively He does; through you and within you!

If you have ever held the role of parent, haven't you taken great joy in playing with your children? Or, if when observing their play or efforts, you provide wise council when it looked like they may end up going in the wrong direction? Do we not as parents take great joy in our children's accomplishments, even if we were not directly involved in those achievements? We take great joy because we know in large part that they succeeded because they heeded the life lessons we taught them, and then those lessons became part of the DNA of their character. Those life lessons and character traits lead to the development of a person of integrity and faith, which helped develop their wisdom and right knowledge and the will to use that knowledge properly, which would ultimately lead to their successes in life.

Would not God take great joy in our efforts to ensure a just man does not die unjustly in their innocence and that a wicked man does not survive and endure in their wickedness? Would not such a creature of such great love of justice and peace aid us in our efforts to ensure justice and peace?

Qoheleth says: vv. 16 "Be not just to excess, and be not over-wise, least you be ruined." Personally, I fear the excessively just person, and I fear it in me. In the age of the internet and social media, I have seen to my dismay the justice of the crowd, the righteous indignation and harsh justice sought by those who have been unjustly harmed. I have seen the innocent few suffer the vengeful justice of the many who condemn, based on popular opinion and the crowd mentality. Human justice seems to have a hard time including mercy and forgiveness in its sentencing of a person who has done wrong. If there is a person who has not done wrong to another person in this life, I haven't met them yet. Yet, when we do wrong and are caught, and cannot deny or hide our misdeeds, we cry for understanding and mercy. Mercy for me, dear God, but not for that man hiding behind the tree!

I came up with a saying about justice many years ago when I noticed how the sinner and the sinned-against reacted to an injustice. It's been a fairly consistent observation throughout my life. It's this:

The guilty ask for mercy, and the victims demand justice. Ah, there's the rub (sorry Will)! Where do we find the balance? Vengeance is mine, sayeth the Lord! I will not be a hypocrite about justice. If someone hurt or killed any of my family, I would cry out to God for justice. I would also be very capable, emotionally, to deliver that justice myself, which could easily turn to vengeance and violence. I fear that side of me and despair somewhat, knowing of the type of violence I'm capable of if I don't put my trust into God's hand for the proper amount and level of justice.

So the previous statement brings me to grace; God's actual, true grace to be specific. By actual grace, I mean God's direct, immediate intervention in the process of justification, and for me, my immediate need for His overwhelming blessing and presence in order that I might not use violence in vengeance to justify vengeance as justice. There may very well be times in our lives when an injustice is so great that we cannot and will not control our actions to address the injustice, and we have set our heart, mind and will to vengeance. That is, unless we have outside help to hold us back, and in our grief and anger, to hold us in a loving presence so overwhelming that we can do naught but allow its presence to hold, to heal, to console, to accept fully our grief and anger, and most importantly to calm the grieving soul so that we do not give in to hatred and violence.

For me, without God's grace, I would succumb to that need for violence and vengeance disguised as justice served. I am not that noble or of strong character. The US Marine in me wants justice, and he wants it now! I cannot give myself God's grace. I can only ask for His grace, and sometimes in an emergency He gives it to us before we even think to ask because it is what we need so as to not fall into eternal darkness of thought, spirit, and deed. Please understand I am not speaking to just accepting an injustice. One should use all that they have at their disposal to receive the justice needed and required in order to heal properly. I am speaking directly about giving in to hatred from the wrong received and the desire for violence as a tool for vengeance, not justice.

My prayer for all who suffer injustice is that we all remember in the midst of our pain and suffering to ask for God's immediate and actual grace to overwhelm us in His presence and love that even before the tears stop and the anger subsides, we can through God's loving grace begin to heal in body, mind, and soul. Amen.

I would like to add one final comment and thought on justice. I have found that mercy and forgiveness is more easily given if the guilty party does pay a price for the injustice they conceived. As William Shakespeare so wisely observed, those who are the recipients of an unjust act, perceived or real, want "their pound of flesh." For human beings, perhaps even more than God's mercy which is beyond human understanding, being sorry, even truly sorry, is not enough to warrant forgiveness. We want our pound of flesh. The wrongdoer must pay for what they did. If the guilty suffer, then somehow it is justice; it is payment for our suffering.

Forgiveness without asking for punishment is hard to come by in a human heart treated unjustly. Yet, time and time again over the years I've marveled at people of faith who unconditionally forgive their transgressors. It happens more often than not with people of faith, a grace-filled people, a religious people. They are my faith heroes. Their showing of mercy and forgiveness draws me closer to an unfathomable God of mercy and love. Their actions and their words of forgiveness humble my spirit. My lofty spirit is brought down to a humble spirit as I see God's Word and way acted in real time by real people of faith who could have just as easily succumbed to their grief and sorrow and rightly demanded only justice. In them, I see a people of God, and I see God in action, not just in thought and contemplation. May we be ever so blessed to be part of such a people. Amen.

When I read the word over-wise, I did not understand its meaning at first. I had to look it up. The definition given was: excessively wise; too clever for one's own good." It also means to not actually listen to God's Holy Spirit and to depend on one's own strength, and to attempt to be too shrewd, intelligent, or perceptive. Too be overly wise in youth and sometimes middle-age is common, and I've come to expect it as a rite of passage into wisdom. To be overly wise in old age is a disaster, especially when the young, thinking that older people know better than they, ask for advice that on the surface may seem wise but is actually akin to a chicken asking a fox how they can best protect themselves from predators.

Over wise; been there, done that, and on occasion slip back into it with almost always the same results as when I was younger. That is; the joker is the one being joked, the deceiver is deceived, and the smart one ends up looking dumb.

Not to overly think this one through, I'll just say this: speak the truth as you understand it with honesty and integrity, say what you mean and mean what you say, do what you said you'd do and not what you'd like to do or would have done, if only. Speak less, listen more, and you'll end up being seen as wise, intelligent, and having an inner strength of character that everyone wants but not all can attain to. And as Stan Lee the creator of many Marvel Comic Book Superheroes was known to say: "Nuff said!"

"Wisdom is a better defense for the wise man than would be ten princes in the city, yet there is no man on earth so just as to do good and never sin" vv. 19–20. There are many of us who are enamored of the rich and the powerful. We tend to see them as having it all. We see them as movers and shakers of the world. Whether they are kings, queens, princes, presidents, or titans of commerce, we tend to think that if we had access to them, we could be protected from bad influences. Their power, rather than God's power and saving grace, would save us. And maybe, just maybe, a little of that power and wealth would rub off on us! Then we wouldn't even have to rely on the rich and powerful because we'd be able to take care of ourselves. Why we wouldn't even have to bother God for help!

Are you getting the sense of arrogance on our part yet? One only needs to watch and read the daily news to see the rich and powerful fall by the wayside time and again. Their riches didn't save them; their power didn't save them. All their defenses didn't save them. Despite all those riches and power, their own hubris brought them down low. Another takes their place as Qoheleth is fond of pointing out.

It is really only wisdom gained from God that is a person's best self-defense. For wisdom, as Ecclesiastes has noted time and again, is having the correct knowledge and its proper application. Proper words and correct actions at the right time have saved many an endangered human being. Since we cannot always have the right knowledge and know the correct action for every situation, we recognize that we often need outside help. Most of the time that knowledge and right action comes from outside help in the way of accessing counselors and experts in their fields.

Sometimes, however, there are situations that no human being can help us with. Most of those times are in times of emergencies. That's when we need to call in the big guns; we need to cry to God for salvation. I have cried to God often in an emergency. Once in my youth, I was swimming with my brothers in Black River in New York State. I dove into a fast-moving portion of the river and got sucked into an undertow. I was being banged against the rocks and could not reach the surface. I was about to panic and probably would have drowned had I not had the sense to ask for help, silent cry that it was. Suddenly I was overwhelmed with a calming presence, and although I heard no distinct words spoken, the presence indicated to me to calm down and ride out the undertow, and it would spit me out further down the river. That's exactly what happened. That was my actual experience of "actual grace" and, given the emergency, wisdom to ask God for help.

I have asked for God's grace and wisdom in other situations in my life, not so dramatic but just as serious. My prayer for you is that you have the wisdom to ask God for help in an emergency and have the wisdom to discern what you need to do or not to do in order to save yourself or your loved ones. Amen.

"(Yet there is no man on earth so just as to do good and never sin" v. 20. I can find no argument under heaven or earth to refute that last part of the statement, yours truly included. There have been entire books written on what to do when one sins and a person recognizes they have sinned and thus have separated themselves from God's presence. They are written a lot better than I ever could. With tongue firmly planted in cheek, may I suggest reading the Bible as a good place to start! P.S. If by some wild chance you actually believe you've never sinned, I'd like to request a seat in the audience on the day of final judgment. It should prove to be a most interesting conversation between you and God.

"Do not give heed to every word spoken least you hear your servant speaking ill of you, for you know in your heart that you have many times spoken ill of others" vv. 21–22. Ah, office gossip, what would we do without it! Full disclosure here, folks. I don't like to spread gossip, but boy do I like hearing it! I honestly believe that it would almost be impossible for human beings to be the social creatures we are if we didn't gossip, well, on just about everything and everybody! I guess I'm not the best spokesperson for this bit of wisdom am I? Still, I have seen the destructive nature of gossip over the years, and I have trained my mouth to speak less and listen often when it comes to gossip. I've even been able to on occasion to turn away from some juicy tidbit of gossip. I've even asked people not to tell me something negative about a person I know because I "fear my servant (read "friend") speak ill of me." In this overwhelming world of digital interconnectedness, I dread reading something online that someone said of me on something I did or said long ago or even just a little while ago. God forgives and forgets, but the internet never does! Ouch!

That fear of ill talk about me keeps me off of Facebook, Snapchat, and the rest of those social media networks. If you need to get hold of me, I have e-mail, and a telephone with internet and text access, and even that took a few years behind the digital curve and divide before I accessed them. OK, Boomer, get with the program!

It's interesting to observe Qoheleth's wisdom on the idea of holding your tongue in the age of digital social interaction on a global scale. When the digital social network was in its infancy, it seemed like a pretty good thing. The sharing of knowledge and experiences was seen as a positive. Then came the birth of digital gossip, and soon everyone had an opinion on just about everything. That seems to have morphed into the idea that the only opinion that matters is your own and only those who think and act like you do. Now it's beginning to look like no one's opinion matters except your group's opinion. Instead of interconnectedness between people, silos of social grouping have begun to form.

There seems to be an emerging trend to all this negative opinion sharing and gossiping. Many of the early adopters and many people of influence have begun to sign off on those social platforms. What was thought to be the sharing and revealing of one's own unique individuality in a spirit of openness and love was beginning to drown in a sea of sameness and meanness. In some good ways, there has been a backlash on the meanness and people are being called to account for their words. Yet if the internet is beginning to teach the world anything about the power of words to come back and haunt you (i.e., your servant/friend/enemy speaking ill of you) it's doing it quite well, and the power of silence and holding one's tongue and thoughtful conversation may yet emerge.

> "All these things I probed in wisdom. I said, "I will acquire wisdom"; but it was beyond me. What exists is far-reaching; it is deep, very deep: who can find it out? I turned my thoughts to knowledge; I sought wisdom and reason, and I recognized that wickedness is foolish and folly is madness." vv. 23–25

God has made a universe so vast that we will never know everything there is to know. We are a child holding a bucket of ocean water, trying to understand and know all there is to know about the ocean. Perhaps God smiles at our efforts. Science with its telescopes has shown us that our physical universe is indeed far-reaching— far-reaching to the point that we have yet to discover its end or even if it has an end. There are stars and galaxies into the trillions, not the billions. There are planets probably too numerous to count around those stars. They are unending. Qoheleth is right, even never having seen what modern man has been able to see with the advancement of science and technology. Our universe is indeed far-reaching, and deep, very deep, and we will never ever find it all out.

Yet God has placed within us an insatiable curiosity to try and know and to understand the deep things of the universe and for the spiritual person to probe the deep things of God. The journey to know, the journey to discover on this plane of existence, is never-ending. Each generation adds knowledge and understanding to the next generation in an unbroken chain of discovery and exploration. It was especially so when we learned to write down our thoughts and discoveries. God even put within our hearts the desire to know Him, the unfathomable, the deep, the very deep, the ultimate unknowable. Some hear His call more than others and eagerly seek Him out. Some are deaf to His call altogether and go about their lives satisfied with what life has set before them. Others hear a still, quiet sound in the back of their minds, deep within their souls, as if calling them to something more than what life has set before them. The voice is unclear, but the "soul-sound" persists, it does not fade away, no matter how annoying it seems to the person who hears and senses it only vaguely.

Then somehow it happens, the vague soul sound, that vague sense of another within calling more earnestly, more clearly: "Come to Me and be fulfilled." Perhaps there was a traumatic event in your life which opened up your soul's ears to hear God's calling you to intimacy with His Spirit. Or, perhaps, it was the simple passage of time with its abundance of experiences that slowly leads to a realization that something, someone, greater than yourself, was calling out to you. No matter how you came to that moment, whether you realized it or not, you would be forever changed and challenged. From that moment on, in one way or another, your spiritual journey had begun in earnest. He will challenge and test you for the sincerity of your heart. The journey will not be a bed of roses, but no other journey will be so self-fulfilling.

Chapter 7

There is no one in the heavens or on earth so far-reaching, so deep, so full of wisdom and knowledge as the Lord God of heaven. He is the ultimate Creator of all that is, of all that we see before us and even beyond, to things no sight, no hearing, no taste or smell or physical touch will ever comprehend or understand without the Creator willing it and revealing it to you. I revel in this gift of life God has given me. I "trip the light fantastic" at the marvelousness of it all. I am a wide-eyed child in a garden and playground of this existence. My mind dances with exploration, it sings in unbridled joy to understanding. My soul caresses the act of creation like an immortal young lover. One touch, one caress of life with all its complexities, it deepness and vastness will never be enough. I have fallen in love with this thing called life and have no desire to leave her, for she is my heart's desire. But I will leave her sooner or later, and my only hope is that I leave her for Him who will return her to me in a way I could never comprehend and in a manner most marvelous.

What a creation this universe is! What a Creator of this marvelous universe! How I long to see and be reunited to Him. All life for me has meaning through and within Him. As much as I love this life, it pales in comparison to wanting to love and be loved by my Creator. How deep are His thoughts and His ways! A person will never fully understand or comprehend them, but I desire to find and have the fullness of my existence in them. For I personally believe that whatever knowledge and understanding I seek and that I need will never be fully found except through Him, in Him, and with Him in the unity of the Holy Spirit, both now and forever.

Eternity is long, my friends, and the universe is wide, vast, and deep. It's going to take a long time to explore it. Let us join with God as the Captain of our "soul starship" and explore together on perhaps a never-ending journey of spiritual growth, love, and learning. Amen.

Critique of Sages on Women:

> More bitter than death I find the woman who is a hunter's trap, whose heart is a snare and whose hands are prison bonds. He who is pleasing to God will escape her, but the sinner will be entrapped by her. Behold, this have I found, says Qoheleth, adding one thing to another that I might discover the answer which my soul still seeks and has not found: One man out of a thousand have I come upon, but a woman among them all I have not found. Behold, only this I have found out: God made mankind straight, but men have had recourse to many calculations. vv. 26–29

A real sage wouldn't touch the idea of the insincerity of women with a thirty-foot pole, let alone a ten-foot pole. I certainly don't think I'm up to the task. In fact I think it's a bit disingenuous for men to even say such a thing. Let's explore a little historical context to his statement and why women might just have had to be not so much as insincere as to be protective of their hearts and their mouths. First off, women were given away by their parents. They had no say so in the marriage arrangement. You got who you got as a husband. If you got a good husband who came to love you sincerely, great! Didn't get the man of your dreams? Tough luck, you just have to stick it out for the rest of your life.

Oh, did we mention you might be the wife with many other wives, for the one man? Did we also forget to mention the concubines? It's starting to get a little crowded around the table and the marriage bed folks! A husband could even sell his wife into slavery and his children in order to pay a debt? Yikes! Then there's divorce. It was easy or at least easier for a man to dismiss his wife (i.e., divorce her) than for a woman to divorce an abusive husband. A woman who was divorced in those days was destined for poverty, as well as her children if the husband dismissed the children with her. A woman could also be legally beaten by her husband for some imagined or real indiscretion. In some cases, a woman could be killed for what she didn't do or did do, or said or didn't say.

Study the Word of God? That was a man's job. A woman was chief cook, baby maker, and breast feeder. You could be a seamstress and maybe a healer of sorts, but not a full-fledged doctor. Not much in the way of a career choice was available back then for women. Even up to this century in some religions, if a woman was raped it was her fault, not the man's. "She seduced me!" was the most common refrain. If a man strayed from the marriage bed, well, he's just doing what comes naturally. A woman who strayed from the marriage bed got stoned to death. The man who strayed with her might get off with a fine or a whipping, but would rarely, if ever, face death.

Anyone getting a sense now, on just why a woman back then might not be sincere of heart, or at least protective of speaking what her heart and mind truly felt? It was downright dangerous to do so if a woman's thoughts and beliefs ran counter to the cultural norm or her husband's. Fear of death, losing access to resources, her children, or receiving a beating is a strong reason not so much as to be insincere as to perhaps hold one's tongue about how one really felt or what they truly believed in. Self-preservation is a strong motivator for hiding one's true feelings and thoughts.

Is it any wonder then that a woman back then, at the bottom of the power pyramid, would choose to use the one tool of power, perhaps the one weapon of destruction at her disposal to disarm a man who might do her harm; her touch, her body, which men have always desired? So is her touch a snare, her body a trap for the weak-willed man? Yes, or a blessing to and for the man who truly loves her. It is men then who must see women as more than something to possess or consume in passion's embrace. It is men who must see and treat women as equals and partners if they are to not see them as Qoheleth saw them those thousands of years ago.

If there is any truth to the idea that women as a whole are insincere, then men should take a really long hard look at themselves, and how they see and treat women as partners and equals, not as property to do with as they see fit. Human beings, men and women, will be open and honest if the environment they are brought up in and live in is an open and honest one. Men must take the log that is lodged in their own eye about honesty, insincerity, and their own sexual desires before complaining about the splinter of insincerity in a woman's eye, especially if it's because a man put it there.

May all men and women be as Adam and Eve before the Fall.

CHAPTER 8

Critique of Sages on the Wise Man and the King:

> Who is like the wise man, and who knows the explanation of things? A man's wisdom illumines his face, but an impudent look is resented. Observe the precept of the king, and in view of your oath to God, be not hasty to withdraw from the king; do not join in with a base plot, for he does whatever he pleases, because his word is sovereign, and who can say to him, "What are you doing?" 8:1–4

HOW DOES SOMEONE recognize a wise person? Is there a PhD attached to their name? Does mere knowledge equate to wisdom? Are all rich and powerful people wise because they are rich or powerful? Are all older people wiser than younger people? I believe that most of us can recognize that neither education, power, wealth, or, the gaining of years will equate to a person being wise. All of those outside indicators will never be a guarantee that a person is wise. That is, a person who knows how to effectively use the knowledge they have at the proper time and place for the proper reason in order to achieve a good certain effect or goal.

There are indicators or characteristics that all wise people tend to have to indicate that they are, indeed, a wise person. Listed below are some of the characteristics that you can observe in a person to determine if they have wisdom.

Wise people can admit they are wrong and thus are open to learning from their mistakes and experiences. They can adjust their beliefs and actions in order to use the insight they've gained properly.

A wise person will not always assume that they are right. They will truly listen to another person's point of view and look for truth in that person's statement as they understand it.

A wise person is most often humble. A wise person does not have an inflated ego. They will have a steady, sure ego, balanced by experience and insight.

A wise person can also take insults better than the average person. They are sure enough in who they believe themselves to be, but not arrogantly so, so as to ignore most insults to their person.

A wise person will understand that sometimes in life they will play the fool before they gain wisdom. I'm something of an expert on that one!

A wise person is very observant of life. They are able to notice the little things in life that most people miss. They understand how important those little things are in the scheme of life and of the subtle effects they can have on living. Because they are observant, they will often first listen and look before speaking.

A wise person loves to learn. They never stop learning. On a side note, from personal experience working in a nursing home for almost eleven years, I consistently observed that the happiest elders were ones who were constantly trying to learn new things. School was never out for them.

A wise person can accept change better than most because they've come to realize that the only constant in a human life is change.

A wise person is not overly concerned with material possessions, but probably does appreciate the finer things in life. They're just not obsessed with obtaining them.

When a wise person gives advice, it's usually grounded in experience and understanding and usually is helpful to the person asking for the advice. They will try and tell you what you need to know, not what you'd like to hear.

A wise person is often compassionate and is loathe to judge another person's actions or reasons for doing so. That's because they do not enjoy being judged either.

Those are some of the few attributes of a wise person. Let's now go to the impudent person. The dictionary defines an impudent person as someone who is marked by contemptuous or arrogant boldness and has an almost total disregard for other people. What are some of the traits of an impudent person?

The impudent person tends to be shamelessly bold and disrespectful to others.

They are immodest. They like to "blow their own horn," so to speak. Everything is about them, and anything that doesn't feed into that narrative is either unworthy of attention or only worthy of scorn.

A person who is impudent is said to lack discretion because they are bold beyond reason. People tend to see them as braggarts and being without wisdom, meaning they do not show good judgment, especially when humility is called for.

Most of us can immediately spot an impudent person and judiciously act to minimize our interactions with them. Qoheleth's main point is that such a person is not looked upon positively by a person in authority over them. At some point in their interaction with such people, the person in authority may sense a challenge to their authority from such a person and come to resent such a person. If a person of authority over you comes to resent you because they see you as challenging them, they may use their power and authority to make your life miserable.

The rest of Qoheleth's comment has to do with the proper attitude when engaging with a person in high authority. He also speaks to the idea of not talking behind the back of a person in high authority and of making sure that you do not seek to undermine the efforts of the person in high authority. Such actions can bring down the wrath of such a person on the scheming, impudent person should the person in high authority discover what they were doing behind their back. Granted Qoheleth uses the term most relevant for his time: "king," but king can easily stand in for any person who has authority over our comings and goings and that which we are charged to do (i.e., work).

"He who keeps the commandment experiences no evil, and the wise man's heart knows times and judgements; for there is a time and a judgement for everything" vv. 5–6. This sentence has more to do not with keeping God's commandments only, but also with keeping with the wishes of the person in authority over you. It basically boils down to the idea of doing successfully what you were asked or told to do, and you will not run afoul of authority, whether it be a man or God.

As I contemplated that idea, I struggled with it because it is somewhat incomplete. As adults in the world of work, I think many of us can probably recall a time or two when we did what we were commanded to do, and we were successful. Unfortunately there ended up hell to pay because we were successful but that which we were asked to do wasn't the "right thing" to do. The person in authority asked for something they shouldn't have and because they had authority over the purse strings of the person (i.e., salary, income, promotions, career, etc.) who had to carry out the edict, that person did indeed carry out the request to everyone's detriment.

Since this book is about biblical wisdom, that is, God's wisdom, my only solution to my conundrum of when to obey or not obey the edict of a person in higher authority was to revert to or refer back to the highest authority: God's edicts, as presented to mankind through the Ten Commandments and the Golden Rule of "Do unto others as you would have them do unto you." Human orders from above may have the legal authority to be implemented, but they must always be weighed against the idea of whether they are just edicts. Slavery was a legal edict. It had the full power of the authority of the justice system in America. It was not, however, a good moral or just law, and people of conscious either passively or actively fought against that law. It is estimated that around three-quarters of a million people paid the ultimate price during the American Civil War to either eliminate that law or to keep it. Justice prevailed, and the law was eliminated but not without the sacrifice of blood.

Most of us will never be asked to make such a hard choice and ultimate sacrifice. Most of our orders from those above us in authority should be carried out with fidelity and conviction for our good and for the good of the organization we work for and with. There will be times, however, blessedly few we hope and pray they may be, when we must ask for the grace of God and the courage and will to do His will; to do what we know deep within our hearts is the right thing to do even if it comes with the highest gift a person can give God: sacrifice.

The last part of the sentence harkens back to Ecclesiastes 3:1, "there is an appointed time for everything, and a time for every affair under the heavens." When it comes to following the orders of those in authority over us, let us pray and hope that the wise person within us, through the teachings and grace of God, will guide the path of our choices to be the right one, at the right time, and for the right reason.

> "Yet it is a great affliction for man that he is ignorant of what is to come; for who will make known to him how it will be? There is no man who is master of the breath of life so as to retain it, and none has mastery of the day of death. There is no exemption from the struggle, nor are the wicked saved by their wickedness 8:6–8.

Yes, we are all ignorant, wicked and good alike, of what is to come. We have written of this dilemma in earlier chapters. Except for the sad act of suicide, there is no escaping our unknown futures. There is no exemption from the struggle of life and death. There is no real exemption from the struggle of trying to make a future we are masters of. There are two ways to deal with the knowledge, that despite all our best efforts, our future really is unknown.

We can give in to despair, throw up our hands, and say: "It is God's will, how can I do anything about it? It's our destiny to live and die on a day not of our choosing." That gives us the potential excuse to do nothing. It allows us to sponge off of other people for our emotional and physical sustenance. After all, what difference do my actions have if I cannot see where my actions lead—to life or death? For me, to give up, to do nothing, and just accept what life sends my way, to give in despair that nothing I do matters, is a living death. I would become a "soul-zombie." I would be a walking, talking nobody, a nothing, moving about the living like a ghost of the damned.

I think all of us have better things to do in life than to obsess about something we have no real control over. Instead, I think most of us have chosen the paths of hope, faith, and love. Those paths are not destinations in and of themselves, but they are the paths to something greater. They led me, however haphazardly, to communion with God. They led me to love people other than myself. They led me to learn new things and to try and use that new knowledge in a useful way. They led me to acceptance that I had no say over my birth nor will I have any say over my death. But they do and did leave me with the desire to fill in the time between birth and death with as much living as possible.

Each new day brings with it the great unknown. We can become a creature of habit and stifling routine in order to give us a false sense of security. Habit and routine can give us the illusion of control, but sooner or later God's unique gift of the unknown knocks on our door. Whether we answer it or not, it will enter of its own free will. If we must face it, let us face it with faith, hope, and love and with God. That is a destiny I can live and die with.

The Problem of Retribution:

> Meanwhile I saw wicked men approach and enter; and as they left the sacred place, they were praised in the city for what they had done. This also is a vanity. Because the sentence against evil doers is not promptly executed, therefore the hearts of men are filled with the desire to commit evil-because the sinner does evil a hundred times and survives. vv. 10–12

The problem of evildoers not being punished at all and even being praised for what they did is as old as man's sense of justice and injustice. Nothing can bring a person's blood to boiling as the perception of someone who is guilty of something being let off, being not charged, or of not being found guilty of the crime they were accused of. As discussed in chapter 7, it can lead a person who has experienced an injustice to allow their anger to cross over to hatred and hatred into acts of vengeance. It is also observed that "as the king goes, so do the people." If people see their leaders doing corrupt and evil things and they do not see justice, they can end up succumbing to those ways in order to just survive. The common refrain we've all used at one time or another in our lives to justify and unjust action is: "Everyone else does it; I may as well also." It especially seems so when it comes to stealing. Somehow it's become a human commandment, overruling God's commandment to not steal, that "if I don't get caught, then it's okay."

My stealing days were for the most part in my early youth. I was cured of the urge to steal very quickly. When I was about twelve or fourteen years old, I went into a department store in Utica, New York, called The State Street Mill. The building used to be a clothing manufacturing building in the late nineteenth century. My grandfather, Joseph Hovish used to work there on the looms. On a shelf was a box of liquid black shoe polish. As an incentive to buy the shoe polish, the shoe polish company had put in a couple of Tootsie Rolls and a plastic ring. I took out the Tootsie Rolls and the plastic ring and closed back up the box and put it on the shelf. I started to leave the store and was caught by the store's undercover security guard. Boy, the fear level of that early teen boy would have shot me to the moon on adrenaline alone! They called my dad who came and picked me up, and we went home. Normally, for something like that I would have gotten a whipping and that would be that.

Not this time. Oh no, the punishment was much worse. I would rather have been hit by a belt than suffer the punishment my dad meted out to me that day. This was the early 1960s, the Silver Age of Marvel Comics. Under the back porch, I had a box with my comic book collection. I had single-digit issues of Spiderman, The Incredible Hulk, and Daredevil in his yellow costume, X-Men, the Fantastic Four, the Avengers, Thor, and a few DC comics as well. There were probably 250–400 comics in all. In the comic book craze of the 1980s and 1990s, that collection would have been probably worth $10,000.00-plus.

My dad didn't hit, he didn't preach to me, he didn't admonish me. He just looked at me and started ripping them all up in front of me. Oh how I cried. I could have probably filled up the bathroom sink with my tears of anguish! The pain, the pain, oh how horrible the pain, as my beauties were destroyed before my very eyes! When it was all said and done, he again didn't say a word. He just got up and went back inside. I was left grieving over my precious collection, now ripped up into dozens of pieces.

Many people I've told the story to over the years said that was too harsh a punishment. It didn't fit the crime of stealing a couple of Tootsie Rolls and a plastic ring. They would roll their eyes when they thought about the monetary worth that those comics would have brought years later. I would have agreed with them except for one odd thing. The punishment worked. In my young boy's mind, the punishment was so horrible all I could think about was that if is this is how I'm punished for two Tootsie Rolls and a plastic ring, just imagine what my punishment would be if I did something worse!

I never stole again. I could not, would not, relive that moment of pure childhood anguish ever again. I was tempted through the years but have pretty much stayed the course. Even when I worked for the NYS Education Department, if I brought home note pads or rubber bands or even paper clips I would feel tinges of guilt if I didn't return them back to the office. Sad to say, there were indeed a few of those things I didn't return over the years, mostly through forgetfulness. Confession, they say, is good for the soul!

On the other side of that equation, I have personally known people who also were of the light finger persuasion who didn't get caught, and who just as Qoheleth pointed out, continued to steal time and again.

The interesting and perplexing thing about doing things that are wrong, and knowing something shouldn't be done, but we still end up doing them because our desires overrule our better judgment, is that knowledge of right and wrong never seems to be able to stop us from doing wrong. Knowledge of right and wrong isn't powerful enough to stop us from doing wrong. Knowledge is not powerful enough to curb our baser desires. Knowledge is not wisdom. It is only one of Wisdom's foundational stones.

I have found only one major power has the ability to overcome, to control, and even to completely eliminate my sinful desires. That power is the active acceptance of God's love for me and in unison with Him, my actively seeking to grow in my love of with, for, and in Him. The more I am able to actively, successfully love God and to allow His love to overpower me and to guide me in right paths, the easier it is to shed temptation in its many forms. No, temptation doesn't disappear, but its hold on me is less strong because I've found something more than those things I previously desired. I've discovered the love of God within me, and I never want myself or anyone else to ever tear it up in front of me, even when my actions put me in danger of losing His love and connection to me. His love for me is too valuable to lose.

"Though indeed I know that it shall be well with those who fear Him; and that it shall not be well with the wicked man, and he shall not prolong his shadowy days, for his lack of reverence to God" v. 12.

It is good to fear the Lord. I can only stand to have so many "comic books" (i.e., read possessions; either physical, emotional, intellectual, and especially spiritual) ripped up in front of me. Fear of the Lord is a reverence for the Lord. He is not a short-order cook of miracles. He's not a concept or great idea. He's a very real presence in my life, a presence I don't fully understand but have come to greatly desire. Unlike the Ring of Sauron; with a nod to J.R.R. Tolkien's Lord of the Rings trilogy, God is not my precious ring of power to be greatly desired for power's sake alone. God's ring of power is His "Ring of Love" which encircles me and holds me tight, yet in a mystery I cannot fully comprehend, His love sends me back out into the world where He asks me to give within my limited abilities and means to point others to that Ring of Love through my meager words and deeds so that His Ring of Love and the power of that love will expand and grow ever larger with each accepting soul.

"Therefore I commend mirth, because there is nothing good for man under the sun except eating and drinking and mirth; for this is the accompaniment of his toil during the limited days of the life which God gives him under the sun" v. 15.

So now Qoheleth reverses his earliest statement about mirth being useless. Although in chapter 2, verse 24, he does say the same thing as the statement above. My Bible footnotes point out that Qoheleth isn't speaking to unrestrained indulgence, but rather legitimate pleasure and cheerfulness that honest toil brings about. It is dining and drinking with friends and family. It is love manifested at mealtime. It is reaping the benefits of your hard work, for honest laughter on life's sillier and confusing moments. It is poking fun at us without being mean about it. It's the type of moments we come to cherish and appreciate for the simple but powerful experiences they are.

Laughter is God's balm against the harsher moments and experiences of life. Laughter softens the blows of hard times. Laughter in the right amount and for the right reason is our secret weapon against despair. Laughter has the potential to speed up healing and to provide hope where there was none before. Above all other types of laughter I cherish, is the shared laughter of good friends and family members.

If you would allow me to go off on a slight tangent but still stick with the subject of humor, it is possible to desire to laugh too much, to use it to hide from life's harsher realities and problems. God knows that I'm guilty of that on occasion. I really, really hate pain of almost any type. I do my best to avoid it if at all possible. Yet over the years, I've learned how to use laughter as a buffer between me and pain. If I can laugh at a hard and serious situation, I can sometimes give myself the breathing room to compose myself and my thoughts and once more enter the breach and work on the problem confronting me.

I really first learned to use that type of humor, which people in the military call "dark humor," from my time serving in the US Marine Corps. Dark humor in the military is everywhere. It is the nature of the military's work to be put into stressful situations. It's making fun of something that isn't actually funny. As far as humor goes, it's not everyone's cup of tea. It's something of an acquired taste. Perhaps the next time you find yourself in a stressful situation, you might want to try it so as to not let the situation overwhelm you.

My prayer for all of us is that may God grant us the gift of honest laughter, good food, good drink, and good family and friends to share it with throughout our whole lives. Amen.

> When I applied my heart to know wisdom and to observe what is done on earth, I recognized that man is unable to find out God's work that is done under the sun, even though neither by day nor by night do His eyes find rest in sleep. However much man toils in searching, he does not find it out; and even if a wise man says he knows, he is unable to find it out." vv. 16–17

A Spiritual Journey into Ecclesiastes

    An ant busy at work does not consider the vastness of the world which it strives to survive in. It does not wonder about the stars and what may be out there. It labors for food shelter, and if lucky enough, reproduction so that irs DNA may be passed onto later generations, ensuring a lasting legacy of its prior existence. People labor for food, shelter, and reproduction. They also labor for love and understanding. They labor for knowledge, never satisfied with what's set before them. Human curiosity is a hungry mouth wide open with no stomach to receive that knowledge and be satiated, and then say: "No more! I now know enough!" So it is with the human soul's desire to know God. We are never satisfied until we are completely in Him and He in us.

    If we're lucky enough to make it to heaven, our souls may finally be satiated with the overwhelming presence of God. We may no longer desire anything but communion with God. No need for science or exploration, for creating or pro-creating. No need for empires and governments. We will be completely satisfied with knowing God by being in His presence. We will probably not worry or concern ourselves with God's work under the sun, the why or how or where of His works.

Mankind will stop searching for understanding the ways of God because he will be in the very presence of God. Or, will mankind continue searching and probing the mysteries of God's ways under the sun; under, perhaps, multiple suns? His ways are deep, His thoughts deeper still, His love vast and overwhelming, and His creations never-ending. Yet this ant still contemplates His thoughts, His ways, and all His creations under the sun. Will those He calls His own, when finally nestled in His eternal embrace of unending love, be truly satisfied? Or, like the fallen angels of long ago who wanted more than what heaven gave them, will mankind once again seek its own way? Will we in some time, where time itself does not exist, seek to leave the Father for other heavens, other dimensions?

I am a small man, in a small body, with a small mind, yet my soul cannot stop searching, seeking to understand God's work under the sun. My soul cannot stop seeking communion with its Creator, and it will not be fulfilled or satisfied until it finds its fullness in Him. But I sometimes worry that the ant (i.e. me) in the end, being unable to comprehend and understand that which is before him, will wander off to a place he knew not, a place he did not need, leaving behind everything and The One (i.e. God) he ever really needed.

Chapter 9

All this I have kept in mind and recognized: the just, the wise, and their deeds are in the hand of God. Love from hatred man cannot tell: both appear equally vain, in that there is the same lot for all, for the just and the wicked, for the good and the bad, for the clean and the unclean, for him who offers sacrifice and him who does not. As it is for the good man, so it is for the sinner; as it is for him who swears rashly, so it is for him who fears and oath. Among all the things that happen under the sun, this is the worst; that things turn out the same for all. Hence the minds of men are filled with evil, and madness is in their hearts during life; and afterward they go to the dead. vv. 1–3

The phrase "love from hatred man cannot tell" means he cannot tell divine favor from disfavor. There is a certain amount of truth to this phrase, and there is another truth just beyond its meaning. When we are in the best of times, for those of us who claim a spiritual life, we praise God and thank Him for His blessings, whether those good times are a direct divine blessing or not. Sometimes good things just do happen. We, however, recognize that the best of times can be fleeting, so we give thanks to God for them. But spiritual people are sometimes disingenuous about their praise to God for His blessings. In the back of our minds, we're hoping by praising God for the good times, He'll, as the song says: "Let those good times keep on rolling!" We recognize on a deeper level that even despite our best efforts we do not have total control to keep those good times rolling.

We also recognize as spiritual people that we are indeed dependent on God for many of the good things that enter our lives.

Some people however, are consciously raised as children to not be dependent upon anyone, even God. We are taught the less you have to rely on others, the better off you will be. The myth of the "rugged individual," who says "Do it my way or the highway," rears its ugly head. This aversion to interdependence is counterintuitive to how children are actually raised. Children are totally dependent upon their parents and if lucky enough, extended family members and friends. Independence of thought and action is gradually introduced over time as children gain experience and wisdom from their thoughts and actions. If a child is lucky enough, they have a parent or parents who gently guide them in their thought processes and evaluation skills. They teach them the value of relationships, which by their very nature are interdependent, not independent.

Even when we leave home as young adults, we will still go back home for advice, support, and comfort when we need or just want it. Then if life presents the opportunity, we get to fall in love with someone else, and then in the throes of love we really, really come to know interdependence. We come to value its fruits, its struggles, and its challenges as life itself reinforces the idea that we are interconnected. We need and want each other. The idea of total independence is I believe counterintuitive to how I believe God wants us to interact and live with each other in peace and harmony.

Then, as it often does in our lives, come the bad times, the hard times, and then confusion of thought and faith take center stage. Is this God's punishment for something I did or didn't do? Am I being punished for the sins of my parents? We may ask; "Is God testing my faith?" Fear and doubt clouds our thought process as we try and cope with hard times. We may become angry with God, thinking we're being "punished" unfairly. We protest our unfair treatment and seek immediate healing.

Hard times and emergencies make prayer come front and center for we who call ourselves spiritual people. We pray, almost in frenzy, for the ordeal to end. I call them the "emergency prayers." We often pray hard to avoid the hard time altogether, to either get around it, over it, under it, or to have it obliterated completely. If we become humble enough and clear-eyed enough, we pray for the strength to get through the ordeal. We pray to be able to face the hard times head on. We pray for God's grace to be with us, to not abandon us during our time of trial.

If we're lucky enough, and yes, even blessed enough, we come out of the ordeal better than we were before. We come away with a renewed sense of what's really important in life, and we adjust our words and actions based on the newly gained wisdom. Then again, sometimes we do not come out a better person for having experienced our ordeal. We are, in essence, broken. We are broken in mind and spirit, and oftentimes in body as well. For me, that's when the real need for emergency prayers comes in. Some healings are never complete. Some pains are never forgotten. It is in those most trying of times that our souls cry out to God in anguish for the help that can only come from Him.

I will say this about direct divine blessings and curses; they are rare. For me, God gives us many blessings just through the process of living, growing, learning, loving, and even in dying. They are the wonderful, average, but very important blessings that God gives all of us, believers and non-believers alike. From birth, to growing pains, to falling in love and even to dying, they are powerful gifts of God, given to all humanity. The earth we walk on, the air we breathe, the water we drink, the food we eat, and the clothes we wear as well as the wonderful people who will come to love us are the powerful and constant blessings of God, but they are not immediate, direct, divine blessings.

These gifts of everyday living are part of the unending cycle of tide and undertow of God's grace that gives birth to the rising high waves of bliss and consolation, as well as crashing waves of despair and hopelessness in the depths of our hearts and souls. When we are given the gift of His healing and consoling grace in such times, we can only gaze on in silent wonder and astonishment on being intimately involved in God's active powers of creation and destruction deep within us, and for our good. For me, a direct, divine blessing or curse, or if you prefer, punishment from God has to do with God's desire to protect us and our relationship with Him, to either enhance the relationship that a direct blessing would bring, even without our asking for the blessing or even understanding that we needed that special blessing. God acts also to protect us from our own bad decisions or outside negative influences that would separate us from Him.

Qoheleth is right, though; we're never quite sure if what is happening to us is God's divine blessing or curse. Absolute knowing is not given to us. We end up acting on faith, hope, and love, or on fear and hatred, and we reap the benefits or detriments those thoughts and actions bring forth from us. May all of us who believe in God and love Him with all our hearts and souls come to accept that whatever our end may be, His real presence will be with us until the end. Amen.

Qoheleth cannot seem to let go of the idea that the fate of all people, good or evil, meet the same fate: death. Death in the Old Testament appears to be the final arbitrator and final experience for human beings of all things. In the Old Testament, once death comes, there is no more. It appears, and not even God stops it for those who led good moral and ethical lives. Thus, Qoheleth's despair, that the good go down to the nether world along with the bad. Qoheleth goes on to write that because there seems to be nothing after death people give into their more basic, animal instincts since there will be no price to pay when we shuffle off this mortal coil. I can agree that some people, neither believing or fearing God, nor believing in a final judgment or an afterlife, have given in to those baser instincts. However, I do not believe in the idea that most people, seeing death as the final fate of all, give in to those baser instincts. As a poster I once saw long ago said: "God don't make junk!" I have personally known atheists, agnostics, and humanists in my short time on earth. I can safely verify that pretty much all of them I met and interacted with haven't given in to their baser instincts. If there was a Hannibal Lector among them, they managed to hide it pretty darn well!

In fact, pretty much the opposite has been true. They recognize the brevity of life, and they recognize instinctually that they need to appreciate the time they have and the relationships they have with family and friends. They recognize that to enjoy the fruit of one's labor, to enjoy a good meal with family and friends are good things unto themselves. Many of them

I've known have added to "the woodpile of life," not taken from it only. They've contributed in a positive way to family, friends, neighbors, and the wider community. If such non-believers, believing that death is the end of all things for those born of flesh, can do good things, and do not give into hopeless despair, how much more, we who claim to believe, should we be doing even more good things?

> Indeed, for any among the living there is hope; a live dog is better than a dead lion. For the living know that they are to die, but the dead no longer know anything. There is no further recompense for them, because all memory of them is lost. For them, love and hatred and rivalry have long since perished. They will never again have part in anything that is done under the sun. vv. 4–6

Indeed, a live dog is better than a dead lion; at least on this plane of existence. No one really knows, not me, you, or Qoheleth, what goes on after death. For me, a person of the Christian faith, I have the hope and faith that death is but a doorway, dark one that it is, to reunion and communion with the Holy Spirit of God. However, I do not unequivocally, scientifically know it. For me, and people like me, it is an "article of faith" that what God said, in the form of Jesus Christ, about a final judgment and an afterlife is true. I have faith that if I truly love God with all my heart, mind, and soul, and love my neighbor as myself, then I will be reunited with Christ, His Father, and the Holy Spirit in heaven; as well as with all the people who preceded me in death whom I've loved and who've loved me throughout my life.

I do not know, nor will I ever know, as in scientifically know, the truth of God's words of assurance to me about and eternal afterlife with Him. I won't even know in dying, if death is the final arbitrator of all things. Dead men don't think or feel anything. No amount of Bible thumping or screaming at the top of my lungs on street corners about God's truth about death, final judgement, and an afterlife will bring me to full knowledge of what happens after death takes us. No amount of quoting the Bible chapter and verse will give me such sure (scientific) knowledge. We do not know, nor will we ever know the truth of God through science. If we wish to be united with Him in spirit, we need to follow the Spirit's rules He's set for us for such a journey. Love and wonder (imagination) leads to hope, hope leads to faith, and faith will lead to the spiritual truth and knowledge of God; a spiritual knowledge, not a scientific knowledge, and I would not have it any other way.

May we travel the road of life to death's door by faith, hope, and love of God and in the prayer, meditation, and application of His holy and living Word. On that Word, we bet our lives; we bet our souls. Amen.

> Go eat your bread with joy and drink your wine with a merry heart, because it is now that God favors your works. At all times let your garments be white, and spare not the perfume for your head. Enjoy life with the wife whom you love, all the days of the fleeting life that is granted you under

the sun. This is your lot in life, for the toil of your labors under the sun. Anything you turn your hand to, do with the power you have; for there will be no work, nor reason, nor knowledge, nor wisdom in the nether world where you are going. vv. 7–10

Finally! Qoheleth finally meets me where I am spiritually about the gift of life and how we are to enjoy it—and enjoy it in the proper way and attitude. May God grant us all such a blessing to enable us to enjoy the fruits of our labors and the fruits of the labors of our hearts. May the Spirit of God shine through you, with you, and in you so that you may follow the deepest, most loving desires of your heart, mind, and soul. May He infuse you with a new way of seeing and sensing the world around you, that you might see and experience God in all living things. May His creative Spirit so overwhelm you that you become a new creation, and in unison with His creative spirit, may you bring new and wonderful things into the world for all to see, admire, and experience. For that creation which comes from God returns to God, but only when it has fulfilled its purpose: to bring you and others into communion with the Most High—Father, Son, and Holy Spirit.

I do have an argument against Qoheleth's final conclusion that there will be no work, or reason, no knowledge, or wisdom in the netherworld. It does not make spiritually logical, or spiritually loving, God-like sense to create a race of human beings made to be loved by Him and for us to love Him and have all the learning, wisdom, and loves gained in this life to be meaningless or nonexistent in the next life. It is roughly estimated that since human beings first became truly physically human beings in mind and body, that 99 billion people have died. That's a lot of dead people with a lot of experiences and accumulated wisdom to ultimately have no purpose. I made two comments in my Bible. The first comment was: "Then why learn in the first place?" My second statement said: "For this life only?" It doesn't make spiritual sense to me.

Some theologians think that when we pass on to the next life, our spiritual communion with God will be so complete that there will be no need to learn anything new; that the ultimate wisdom and knowledge is to be in communion with God. That may be, but God who made us in His image also made us creators, and explorers. He made us questioners of all that is, even of Him. He also made a universe so vast and so full of galaxies and stars and planets that they would seem ripe for exploration and for expanding the name, renown, and Spirit of God throughout the universe, perhaps even on a heavenly plane of existence. There's a good chance I'm probably wrong about the idea that once we are united with God, there will be no need for anything else but communion with God. After all, the saints and prophets all say that all ultimate human fulfillment is to be found in communion with and in the Spirit of God. Somehow, for some oddball reason I cannot pin down, I do not think God will be done with us once we reunite with Him in heaven. For a reason I can only partially comprehend and sense, when we are finally united with Him the real adventure of heaven and earth will begin!

The Evil Time Not Known:

> Again I saw under the sun that the race is not won by the swift, nor the battle by the valiant, nor a livelihood by the wise, nor riches by the shrewd, nor favor by the experts; for a time of calamity comes to all alike. Man no more knows his own time than fish taken in a net, or birds trapped in the snare; like these the children of men are caught when the evil time falls suddenly upon them. vv. 11–12

In these days of the internet, of twenty-four-hour news feeds, and ubiquitous social media posts, this truth is proven over and over again. Disaster comes suddenly, unbidden; sometimes we see it far off and do nothing to stop it even when it is in our power to do so. The impending disaster doesn't match up with our beliefs and values; it goes against our desires, and so we will it away to our own misfortune. When I first started writing this book, three large events were and are unfolding in the news that brang home the truth in Qoheleth's statement. Back in 2019 in China, a virus that became known as COVID-19 began infecting people in the city of Wuhan. And alarm was raised, but no one actually knew how serious the virus would become. When the virus crossed over into America, from Europe, from people who had traveled to China, most probably at the end of 2019 or the beginning of 2020, it was already too late. Since it landed on American shores over 1,000,000 Americans have died from it and over 100 million-plus Americans have been infected by it. At first, it struck the old and medically vulnerable. Eventually it started to spread to all age groups regardless of health condition, including people who had been vaccinated against the virus.

In 2020, various pharmaceutical companies developed a very effective vaccine. Hope was born. Then politics got into what should have been just a health issue. People questioned their government because of past mistakes. They talked about freedom of choice. It has become something of an "us versus them" issue. People began to refuse the vaccine based on personal and religious reasons. The vaccine didn't care about your religious affiliation or personal beliefs or about the efficacy of the vaccine or the trustworthiness of our government. It hasn't stop killing people. In fact it's began to kill mostly the unvaccinated . Disaster and death can be a great motivator to overcome personal and religious beliefs. The news began to forecast that vaccinations were up in those states where the number of vaccinated people was low. Death is once again a teacher of reality.

The sad part of this is that the disaster didn't have to happen at the level it did and is continuing to do. As I mentioned earlier in this book: "We have met the enemy and he is us! " (thank you, Pogo).

The second disaster unfolded in the country of Afghanistan. Back in 2001, a group of terrorists plotted and successfully carried out an attack on American soil, killing almost 3,000 Americans. We successfully invaded the country and destroyed the terrorist group, and years later, we killed its ring leader. We'd been there for twenty years, trying to shore up the government and train their military to defend against and defeat another group, the Taliban, that harbored the first terrorist group. We had hoped to inspire the country with the American way of living and the benefits of democracy. We spent hundreds of billions of dollars in training, military equipment, education, and economic development.

It was all for nothing. We notified the country that we would pull most of our troops out of the country by September 11, 2021, twenty years after the attack on America. The country quickly fell to the Taliban before we even left the country! The well-trained and equipped, combat-air-supported, Afghanistan troops of 300,000-plus against 75,000-plus Taliban gave up without hardly firing a shot. City after city, provincial government after government just surrendered without a fight. Even their president fled. How can troops even try to be valiant when they aren't even supported by the own government? The "experts" predicted they might fall in one to two years. Nobody saw the collapse of the government in under a month. So much for the expert's opinions on the government not falling quickly.

Thirdly, Russia invaded the country of Ukraine and is trying to annex it. Fighting has been raging for ten months with no end of the fighting in sight. True peace, God's peace, seems to always evade us.

Time and again in the news there are stories of financial wizards losing their shirts in the stock market or other investments. Stories abound of very smart people just barely making a living. And, there are stories of the fastest and strongest athletes who seem to lose a race or contest from someone no one saw coming. The saddest thing to experience is the disaster foretold and not prevented when it could have been. God has an odd sense of humor sometimes. I've noticed in my own life that He will on occasion make me the prophet of my own doom, and I've seen it happen to other people also. I will often feel "gob smacked" (God smacked?!) when I predict something about someone or something else, and it happens to me instead. Ouch! It has happened to me on a couple of occasions on issues of health and safety. Luckily for me I have an odd sense of humor and am, for the most part, able to take the turn of events with a grain of salt and defeated shrug accompanied by a wimpy sigh!

My spiritual solution to avoiding disasters as much as possible is a nightly prayer I say to God, asking for His protection. I present it here for your possible use. So far it's been working!

Dear God please protect me, my family, friends, and neighbors from immediate disaster today. Please protect us from a disaster born of chance and the choice of others. I understand You have made me responsible for my own choices. Let us be free today of violence, accidents, and the sudden onslaught of disease. Let us see the length of days You had planned for us since the day we were formed in our mothers' wombs, that at the end of our lives we may give You thanks and praise for allowing us to see the fullness of those days. Thank you for keeping all of us safe yesterday, as we rely on Your help today to keep us safe. May we remember that if disaster does strike, that the rules of chance and choice must be followed, that we then have recourse to Your saving power to overcome any and all crises that come our way. Amen.

The Uncertain Future and the Sages:

> *On the other hand I saw this wise deed under the sun, which I thought sublime. Against a small city with a few men in it advanced a mighty king, who surrounded it and threw up great siege works about it. But in the city lived a man who, though poor, was wise, and he delivered it through his wisdom. Yet no one remembered this poor man. Though I had said "Wisdom is better than force," yet the wisdom of the poor man is despised and his words go unheeded. vv. 13–16*

Qoheleth saw something that is all too common among human beings: non-recognition of people who helped avert a crisis or overcome a dangerous situation. Once the danger has been averted or overcome those in power go back to maintaining their power, prestige, and community status, as if they were the ones responsible for saving everyone. There are several unique dynamics happening in these few sentences. The first one that struck me was that Qoheleth did recognize the poor man's wisdom. The second, which, most probably no one considered, was that Qoheleth is a person of power and he could have done something to publicly recognize the gentleman's wisdom to his community. Then perhaps, because he was a person of power, even higher than the important citizens of the city the poor man saved, he could have caused those officials to have to recognize that person's efforts on the city's behalf. It may seem a bit of a stretch to pull that thought out of his statements. However, I'm speaking from personal experience in that I have observed both circumstances. The first, as described by Qoheleth was someone of low-rank doing something that we would have thought to have been done by a higher social rank leader. Then, once the crisis is over, it's back to normal for everyone, including the hero or heroine of the moment.

I've also observed where a higher up has recognized the efforts and accomplishments of a person on the lower end of the power and status ladder, thereby forcing the people of power below that higher power person to officially recognize that person's efforts and the wisdom that lead to the accomplishment.

With thirteen years in the US Marine Corps and over thirty-two years in a government bureaucracy in some positions of supervisory leadership, I have recognized that the best leaders do consistently recognize staff efforts who are not necessarily high up on the power structure of the organization. Another thing I was able to recognize, which to me does not happen often enough, is that the poor man's city leadership were able to recognize his wisdom and were willing to implement his idea or suggested plan of action. So while we may look disparagingly at the city leadership for not having done more to recognize that person's wisdom and efforts to save the city, we must give them credit for swallowing their own pride at not having been able to come up with the solution and having been willing to implement his plan of action. For many in leadership positions, it is often hard and humbling to admit that the solution to a problem didn't come from them.

Yet, once again the best leaders, the ones we are most apt to follow willingly and even eagerly, are those who recognize that most human endeavors are a team effort. They want others' ideas and solutions. They do not lord their power and prestige over others. The best leaders see themselves as teachers *and* students, and as followers *and* leaders. They do not lock themselves into their own ego's desires. They also recognize and praise publicly the successful efforts and ideas of others. They use the power that is given to them to enhance those who serve him or her.

There are a few other interesting things going on in the background that are not apparent in Qoheleth's words. There is no description of the poor man asking for recognition or a change in status for his importance in saving the city. He saw his city, his community in trouble, and he acted to save it without any idea of being recognized for it. He basically did what was needed to be done and then went back about his usual business. Would he have liked to have been recognized? I'm sure he would have. Most of us would have been happy to have been recognized for such wisdom that saved an entire city from a force greater than the city would have been able to deal with. God, however, does not call us to use wisdom for acts of self-aggrandizement.

For those of us of the Christian faith, the words of Jesus in Luke 17:9–10 should come to mind: "He does not thank the slave because he did the things which were commanded, does he? So you too, when you do all the things which are commanded you, say, 'We are unworthy slaves; we have done only that which we ought to have done.'" So, too, in pre-Christian times as observed in the Old Testament books, even the greatest prophets and kings did the work of God as commanded without considering whether or not they would receive fame and recognition. Because they did so, God greatly honored them and have given them a name and honor that has lasted for thousands of years.

Finally, while Qoheleth doesn't even mention the poor man's name so as to give him the recognition he deserved, God who sees all and is able to explore the deepest intentions of our hearts will remember him by name, and all of us who pass into His heavenly kingdom will know it also.

"The quiet words of the wise are better heeded than the shout of a ruler of fools. A fly that dies can spoil the perfumer's ointment, and a single slip can ruin much which is good" vv. 17–18. A truth softly spoken, with firm conviction, at the proper time, given in love, when it needs to be heard is more powerful and effective than a leader's words whose only voice volume is constantly set on high. As mentioned earlier in this book, the increased decibel of any advice or argument I give will not make it any righter than the actual truth it espouses.

Shouting gets our attention; it does not translate into our approval of what is shouted. There are times for shouting. If there weren't, God wouldn't have given us the ability to shout. In times of danger, shouting may save lives. A well-placed (not constant shouting) shout has stopped many a child from getting into trouble or danger. Shouting is sometimes needed to get our attention; it is not needed and is indeed counter-productive to continue to shout once attention has been gotten.

It's easy to say, but much harder to avoid when you're in a heated argument with your spouse or children (guilty as described!). When our emotions get the best of us, when we feel endangered, when our identities are attacked, when our motives are questioned, turning down the volume can be almost impossible until the anger and fear energy level is depleted. It's like trying to put the overflow of a waterfall into a one-inch pipe. That understanding of the intense energy level due to fear or anger is the key to regaining control of our emotions and our tongues. A disciplined mind and tongue come about when we can recognize that we must redirect that intense energy elsewhere. If we continue to direct our ire at the actual source that gave birth to those intense emotions, we may end up adding fuel to the fire of our emotions and lose total control.

Sometimes the only way to deplete all that negative energy is to leave the scene entirely. This will allow you to deplete it out of harm's way. It may not solve the issue, but it allows the energy of anger and frustration to lose its control over us. Other times, the issue is so important that we must stay and confront the source of our agitation. If that is the case, our first action should be an immediate prayer to God for His grace to overflow within us to help us regain control of ourselves. Then, with God's grace we need to laser focus our words, and if need be, our actions, in order to put our point across and to maintain our honor, dignity, and integrity as children of God. However we confront the shout of a king or queen of fools or the shouting fool within us, let us remember that if we ask, we have recourse to God's saving grace and Spirit so that we are seen as having the quiet words of the sage and not the loud cries of a king or queen of fools.

Now, about that fly in the perfumer's ointment and the single slip that has ruined many a good thing, my Bible doesn't really expound on that. So I'm left guessing somewhat on what it ultimately means. For me, the fly is a metaphor for a negative action or words inappropriately applied to someone's work, efforts, or relationship(s), on something they are trying to accomplish, create or enhance. That negative word or action can cause the destruction and downfall of all the previous good you were trying to do. You could end up as they say, "starting from scratch."

There are easy examples all around us of examples of the fly in the ointment when it comes to physical activities. In cooking, it could be putting in the wrong ingredient or over- or under-cooking something. For a builder, it could be using the wrong materials for the job or using the wrong tools for a job. For the baker, it could be not putting in enough yeast or too much yeast in the dough. We all can recognize those types of situations in our lives. Often, though, it is not the physical flies that mess up our ointment of pleasure. It is often the inappropriate word said to a colleague or a selfish act of ourselves or others that ruins a good thing. For me, my most important example of this fly in the ointment of good has been seen as a parent and as a teacher.

If there any parents who never said a cross word to their children at the absolutely worse time or denigrated a child's efforts on something, I have never met them, and no parent I've ever known has been so bold to believe they never made a mistake with their children. How many of us are stuck in the wrongs of our childhood as adults? We are unable to forget, forgive, or let go of the injustices we endured, especially from those who have loved us the most! They became for us the fly in the perfumed ointment of a happy life.

We often say: "Why, yes, we've forgiven those past injustices and have moved on to happier times and places." Yet, the emotional memory is not forgotten, and forgiveness is more on the lips than in the heart. This does not mean a negative judgment on such a hard reality. When we hurt, we hurt. Our denying that hurt, that pain, doesn't eliminate it. In fact, it only gets worse. There is an unusual truth not pointed out by Qoheleth that can help us, as adults deal with the fly in the ointment of our youth.

That truth, though simple in words, is admittedly, difficult to enact. That is, as adults, that which we did not have the power to do as children is to consciously remove that fly; *not* from our youth, but from our adulthood. Sometimes only God's grace gives us the power to do that. The good news is that God is more than willing to bestow such a powerful gift upon us. We do have to consciously ask Him, though. It doesn't just automatically happen just because He loves us. If you trust and have faith that He will give you such a wondrous gift, *it will happen.*

If you are lucky enough to believe, to have the faith and hope for God's grace to *help, you remove* the power of those childhood painful memories over you and those experiences from your adulthood, then you will experience a freedom of thought and action you might never knew was possible. No longer tethered to a painful past, your present and future becomes wide open with possibilities. The old fears and resentments will be truly dead. There will be memories, but the power they had over you will no longer exist because you accepted the grace of God to heal you.

If ever you receive such a gift of God I hope and pray that in your newfound happiness and freedom of thought and conscious will, that you return your thoughts, your heart, and your prayers of thanksgiving back to God. For while you may not immediately recognize it, God wants to share in your joy and your newfound freedom. And perhaps, because you turned your thoughts and heart to Him, like the poor man in Qoheleth's story, He will enjoy the recognition of His part in freeing the city of your soul, your spirit, from a power and a danger greater than yourself. Normally my statement above would be where I would cease making comments on Qoheleth's words, but there is another important group of people I've felt the need to address about the flies in the ointment of childhood; that is teachers, specifically middle or junior high school teachers. This many seem like a strange place to speak to middle/junior high school teachers, but hear me out.

As someone who has had to monitor and evaluate the federal education program known as Title I, Part A in New York State (NYS) elementary, middle, and high schools for many years, I'd come to realize the importance of middle/junior high school teachers in solidifying the love, hatred, or total indifference of a curriculum subject in pre-teens and early teenagers. Specifically, I used to monitor what is commonly referred to as academic intervention services (AIS) programs. They are additional academic services for children who are failing or struggling academically in the core subjects of mathematics, English language arts (ELA), science, and social studies. Children failing or struggling in other academic subjects could also be provided AIS, but mostly such services were in those four academic areas, with mathematics and ELA taking the larger portion of federal funds for services. Program after program of observations revealed to me the following truths of AIS in public schools in NYS.

The first is the most robust and in-depth services were observed at the elementary level, including the Pre-Kindergarten (Pre-K) level. Teachers, parents, school administrators, and the students themselves were almost always observed at high levels of engagement with the instruction. They wanted to learn, and their parents and administrative and instructional staff wanted them to learn. It showed in the classroom.

The second thing I constantly observed was that by the high school level, especially from tenth grade and up, the high schools were instructing students who had become either really excited about certain subjects, were total indifferent to a subject and just wanted to get through the course to get enough credits so they could graduate high school, or finally had come to actually hate a subject.

Interviews after interviews with staff and students and AIS program observations after observations revealed the middle/junior high school academic truth. Students were either won over or lost to a subject in middle/junior high school. Success in AIS and in the regular classroom depended heavily on the middle school teacher-student relationship.

The actual subject was somewhat irrelevant to a student's success. It was how the subject teacher saw the student's ability to handle or pass a subject, how the teacher felt about the subject they were teaching (positive or negative attitude), and how that student internally translated the subject teacher's attitude toward the subject, and the teacher's attitude about the student that was a strong, but by no means only indicator, if the student was going to take to the subject and be able to pass it.

To be blunt; the middle/junior high school teacher and the classroom environment they created, and teacher's attitude to a struggling student became either the ointment of perfume that helped a student develop a positive attitude to a subject, wherein for many they learned to love a subject, which in the future influenced the career path the student would follow. The alternative was the teacher who became the fly in the subject ointment, and the student either became totally indifferent or actually came to hate a subject. That doesn't say that such a thing does not happen at the elementary or high school level. It does, but the preponderance of interviews and classroom observation showed me that it was the middle/junior high grade level where the public school system won or lost a student's enthusiasm for a particular subject. Without enthusiasm, there is little in-depth learning for much of anything.

My biblical advice is simple: be the perfumed ointment of the subject you teach and hopefully love and be always aware of the personal internal fly of pessimism and indifference that would kill the joy of learning in the very subject you yourself take great joy in. My prayer for middle school teachers, indeed all teachers, is that you become the spark of inspiration that turns on a student's love for learning and for the subject in which you fell in love with many years ago.

All things born of the human heart and mind and brought forth in words and deeds are either perfumed ointment to the heart, souls, and minds of people, or they become the fly, the careless word or deed which spoils all the good it touches. With God at our side, let us all be that perfumed ointment. Amen.

Chapter 10

"More weighty than wisdom or wealth is a little folly! The wise man's understanding turns him to his right; the fool's understanding takes him to his left." "When the fool walks through the street, in his lack of understanding he calls everything foolish" 10:1–3. It would be easy when writing about these passages to admonish the fool who sees everything as foolish and as a waste of time and effort and to praise the wise man's ability to use his wisdom to make the right decisions about the proper actions to take in any given situation, to turn the right way. It might even be fun for me to spout words of wisdom about our need to gain wisdom in order to help guide our life's paths. But the fool in me would be hiding in my supposed words of wisdom about wisdom, for I have found out a harsh truth about the wise and the foolish. Life and God test our true intentions and desires throughout our lives. In that testing, if we are brave enough and humble enough, we come to understand a basic truth about ourselves.

We will play the fool *and* the wise sage. I literally cringe and wince in pain when I recall all the dumb, foolish things that's come forth from this mouth of mine. I tremble with fear as I've come to the realization that life and God will present me with many more opportunities to play either the fool or the wise sage. How I hate the fool in me and greatly desire the wisdom of wise men and women. But desire and hate do not necessarily make either choice a reality. To paraphrase the Great Bard: desire, love, and hate do not necessarily lead us fools to dusty death. But, boy, they sure do try, don't they?

I recognize that love, hate, wants, and desires can become doorways and pathways to wisdom and foolishness. I have treaded those paths enough times to understand the truth of that statement. The mystery for me has always been why I chose the path of the fool rather than the sage. The even-bigger mystery for me is why, having the ability to see the end road of a foolish decision, in essence, being my own prophet of doom, I still actively chose the path of the fool? When I choose to make a foolish decision or statement, I almost instantly lose control of the destiny I want and need, and substitute it for a destiny I did not want nor did I desire.

Wisdom will either flee or admonish the foolish. Sometimes wisdom will even try and totally avoid the foolish. But to paraphrase Plato, we are all fools on a ship of fools, and the four winds blow us as they may. Only if we choose wisdom as the captain of our ship will we gain the helm and rudder that will take us on great adventures and bring us to safe harbors. Yet, that knowledge does not give us wisdom, does it? As I've written before, knowledge of something doesn't make it real. Knowledge is simply the act of opening the door to wisdom's riches.

So where is all of this leading to? What truth have I learned about the gaining of true wisdom? How do I avoid being the fool over and over? For me, on a very personal level, I have come to believe as Qoheleth has stated; that true wisdom comes from the Spirit of God. The living water of the fountain of wisdom, the fruits of the garden of wisdom, the knowledge held in the great spiritual library of heaven, comes from the Spirit of God. Like King Solomon, we must actively choose and ask for wisdom. God gives her to us freely for those who truly seek her.

There is a worldly wisdom that most of us use in our daily lives called common sense that helps us weave through successfully the everyday relationships, experiences, and activities. It should be recognized as the important daily wisdom that it is. It is however limited in scope. It does not lead us to the higher spiritual truths. Common sense does not bring us closer to the Creator; only spiritual wisdom can do that—and that greater wisdom comes only from God.

As I've gotten older, I've made it a habit to pray to God whenever I must make a major decision in life. I ask for His wisdom when I must make the kind of major decision that could lead to happiness or ruin, to wealth or poverty, to just choosing a job or choosing a life-fulfilling career, to a loving relationship or a broken one. God's wisdom, when I actively sought it and received and used it properly, has saved me from many potential disasters and has led me to many material, emotional, intellectual, and spiritual blessings. My prayer for you is that you, too, may seek and receive God's wisdom and its benefits, a wisdom that surpasses human understanding. Amen.

"Should the anger of the ruler burst upon you, forsake not your place; for mildness abates great offenses" vv. 4. Does the phrase: "It's time to face the music" ring a bell? Qoheleth, I believe, is saying that if you've done something wrong that has greatly offended someone who has authority and power over you, it is better to admit one's mistakes and face that person with humility and perhaps even repentance than it is to hide from the consequences of those mistakes or avoid that person in authority. An attitude of humility and repentance will go a long way to easing the anger of the person in authority over you than it would be by hiding from them to avoid the consequences of your actions, or by trying to defend yourself when you know what you did was wrong.

Another common phrase for this situation is: "being called on the carpet." I've been called on the carpet throughout my entire life. I've been called out on the carpet when my words or actions were wrong by bosses, my wife and children, and friends. You might say but some of those people were not necessarily people who had authority over you. I would beg to differ for the following reasons. First, even children have authority over their parents when the parent was wrong and the children were right. The true authority in those situations is actually truth itself, not necessarily the people. If I've said or done something wrong against someone, if I've been the unjust one, the lazy one, or didn't do something I gave my word I was going to do, then my negative actions or words puts me morally and ethically under the person or persons I've aggrieved. The victims of my unkind words or unjust actions have moral authority over me. Qoheleth was really talking only about kings, queens, princes, and princesses and perhaps judges (i.e., royalty and the judicial system). There is no doubt that there are persons in authority over us throughout our lives. To not recognize that would be foolish to the point of our own detriment. I would argue the true authority over our actions and words will be the truth of our words, actions, and inactions.

"I have seen under the sun another evil, like a mistake that proceeds from the ruler; a fool put in lofty position while the rich sit in lowly places. I have seen slaves on horseback, while princes walked on the ground like slaves" vv. 5–7. I believe Qoheleth's observation is based on the idea of someone who is incompetent or not deserving of a position of authority being given such a position simply because they are in the king's favor, or due to a circumstance that has upended the normal order of things. He is also alluding to the idea of those who should be in positions of authority and power being denied their proper position and being put under the authority of someone who is not qualified or competent to be in a leadership position over them.

I think we can all attest to having had someone in authority over us who was not fit for the position of authority and leadership but was there "because they knew someone." Some people, who are that lucky to be given the gift and responsibility of leadership even though they aren't initially qualified for it, will grow into the job. They will seek to learn from others and their experiences. Others, though, will remain the fools that they are. They will spout half-truths and sometimes outright lies. At other times, they will make decisions that will turn into unmitigated disasters. They will show favoritism. They not only put their foot into their mouths, but if it were physically possible, they probably would stuff their leg up to their thigh for added measure!

I wonder, though, would we have the wisdom to know when "we've bitten off more than we can chew?" Have we the ability to recognize that we aren't suited for a particular position of authority, responsibility, or leadership? Would we be wise enough not to seek such a position or, having such a position, to humbly remove ourselves from it so as to not cause more damage to those we are responsible for? Power and prestige is a heady brew for our egos; it is a drink we do not easily put down.

While Qoheleth's comments do not mention it, there is another sin of leadership that should be addressed. It is the person called to a leadership position who has the skills and abilities to take up the mantle of leadership and the responsibilities that come with it; but refuses to do so for selfish reasons. Let's face it, being in a leadership position takes a lot of work; it takes a lot of energy. Sometimes we need to be selfish for our own sanity. There are times we need to decline a leadership role. There are other times that God calls us directly to take up the mantle of leadership because He needs you to be a beacon of light and guidance to people in need. He recognizes that you are the best fit for the leadership role. You are needed as His face in challenging times. There may be many reasons to say no to becoming a leader to people in need, but there is really only one reason to say yes to the invitation—because God asks you to.

"He who digs a pit may fall into it, and he who breaks through a wall may be bitten by a serpent. He who moves stones may be hurt by them, and he who chops wood is in danger from it" vv. 8–9. I'm going to put my interpretation skills at risk here and go out on a limb to suggest that Qoheleth is not saying that we shouldn't dig a pit, break through a wall, move stones, or chop wood. I believe he is saying that with each endeavor we undertake, we need to realize that there are inherent risks to everything we do. We need to be cautious and careful in the things we choose to do. Not all efforts result in physical danger. Some spiritual and intellectual efforts, some financial efforts, and some efforts at building relationships if not done with careful consideration can result in a spiritual, financial, or intellectual snake bite or fallen stone, or a cut from the fallen axe of a broken heart and spirit.

My prayer for us all is that with God's spirit of wisdom as our guide we may approach all of the tasks given to us under the sun, with the time given to us and with the seriousness and thoughtfulness that is due them so that with a clear conscious we may partake of the fruits of our labor and enjoy the work of our hands, hearts, minds, and souls. Amen.

"If the iron becomes dull, though at first he made easy progress, he must increase his efforts; but the craftsman has the advantage of his skill. If the serpent bites because it has not been charmed, there is no advantage for the charmer" vv. 10–11. Qoheleth was pointing out that the expertise of the craftsman would remind him to sharpen his saw every now and then so that he would not have to work twice as hard to do the same amount of work. Sometimes in our busy work lives, we get so focused on accomplishing a task that we forget the real need to stop and reflect on what we are actually doing and accomplishing. In essence, we forget to sharpen our own saw. The craftsman, who is considered an expert at what they do, has a history of that person in a constant state of self-evaluation and continuous improvement. They are not satisfied with the basics of their craft. They want to excel at it; so they study, they compare and contrast, they experiment, they practice, and they consistently make sure to take good care of their tools; whether physical, mental, emotional, or spiritual so that they will last and be even more effective tools for many years.

For the spiritual and intellectual craftsmen, for the social-emotional craftsman, those sharpening-the-saw techniques also apply. Their tools may be different, but both the physical craftsman and the spiritual, intellectual, and social-emotional craftsman must study, compare and contrast, experiment, and practice and practice, and then practice some more. People often marvel at the speed at which an expert can solve a problem or create something of use and/or beauty. The speed at which they made those accomplishments came only with years of constantly sharpening their saws, through trial and error, through multiple failures and successes. They effectively sharpened their saws through hard-won experience. It is wisdom to know when you need to sharpen your saw.

The craftsmen, whether of the physical kind or the more esoteric kind, also know it is important to take care of their human tools related to their physical, social/emotional, mental, and spiritual needs. Such people over time became people of integrity. They are considered "whole people." They see and recognize the importance of maintaining a healthy balance in all aspects of their lives, and it shows in the work they do and by acknowledgment of their peers on the high quality of their work.

If you would like a more in-depth discussion of those human needs I highly recommend Stephen Covey's book: *The Seven Habits of Highly Effective People*. Read his chapter 7 on "Sharpening the Saw." Qoheleth would give it his nod of approval; trust me on this. Another book of Covey's, which I own and reread on many occasions is: *How to Find Your Mission in Life*. He lays out a spiritual guide on how best to find your true purpose in life and in doing so find fulfillment. You can read the book in one hour, but you may get a lifetime's share of spiritual wisdom from it. I can't give it a higher recommendation than that.

On the serpent's bite statement, I have to make a judgment call on its meaning. My Bible doesn't really give an explanation as to its meaning. I believe what Qoheleth is pointing out is that if you have a skill set but don't use it, or don't use it properly, you should fully expect the thing which you could have solved or could have fixed, like the aforementioned serpent, will come back to bite you—usually in the rear end! That little bit of wisdom brings me back to some old folk wisdom I heard long ago which applies here to the serpent biting. That is, the saddest words in the English language are: woulda, shoulda, and coulda. My prayer for us all is that the good Lord's spirit and a good strong shot of motivation and commitment on our part will make us a people of "I will, I did, and it's done!" Amen.

> Words from the wise man's mouth win favor, but the fool's lips consume him. The beginning of his words is folly, and the end of his talk is utter madness; yet the fool multiplies words. Man knows not what is to come, for who can tell him what is to come after him? When will the fool be weary of his labor, he knows not the way to the city vv. 12–15?

Since the idea behind these words have been already discussed early in this chapter, there isn't a lot to add, but being the foolishly wise I make myself out to be, perhaps a few observations can be made to provide food for spiritual thought. Have you ever thought on how often we remember commercials on TV and radio or on the internet more than we sometimes do for hour-long TV shows with multiple shows within a series? Our minds tend to wander after only a few seconds or in just a couple of minutes of someone talking to or worse yet, at us. We remember *Aesop's Fables* better than the tales of *The Knights of the Round Table*. We remember easier parables, such as those told by Jesus, and short stories than we do 1,000-page novels.

So it is when the foolish speak. Words on end have us drifting into daydreams of escapism. So, too, do many words from one smart person in a very long meeting, lecture, or God forbid, homily! How we do like to hear our own thoughts spoken out loud to an audience who may or may not appreciate our dropping pearls of wisdom! This very book is a struggle for me to balance my words of faith and a desire to be heard and taken seriously, without getting too windy. Only you, dear reader will be the ultimate judge as to whether I succeeded or not.

The funny thing about smart people and long lectures and longer homilies is that they don't seem to have a clue that they've pretty much lost most people by the end of twenty minutes. Thank God and science for tape recorders and digital recordings, I guess! Still, despite my jest, I think I've made my point that a few words at the right time, in the right place, by the right person (think Abraham Lincoln's Gettysburg Address) has shown to be more effective than an hour's long discourse on just about anything. Heck, poor St. Paul so bored a young man to literal death while he was preaching (he fell off a window ledge after he fell asleep listening to St. Paul) that he had to bring him back to life! I wonder if St. Paul changed his preaching style after that? Here's hoping St. Paul can appreciate my sense of humor!

I guess the best bit of wisdom we can get from Qoheleth's words on the subject is whether you're a wise sage or a fool, it behooves all of us to know when to shut up and just listen! Here's hoping my few words on the subject of a fool or a wise man and too many words are few enough to get my point across.

Man Does Not Know What Evil Will Come:

"Woe to you, O land, whose king was a servant, and whose princes dine in the morning! Blessed are you O land, whose king is of noble birth, and whose princes dine at the right time (for vigor and not in drinking bouts)" vv. 16–17. Abuse of power by those in authority and leadership positions is a tale as old as when humans first came together in tribal units. There is something about being in a leadership position and its accompanying authority that often, but not always, feeds into human egos to that person's detriment. Such people who think it's almost their birthright to lord it over others tend to accept all the accolades when something goes right and then will blame everyone but themselves when something goes wrong. They are the worst kind of leaders, and over time, people will either ignore them, copy their attitudes in their own work, or fear them for the arbitrary way they wield their power. They will almost never respect them, nor will they follow them into danger, for such leaders abdicate their leadership responsibilities at the first sign of danger to themselves. On rare occasions if the people under their authority do not succumb to their leader's ways and they hold on to their integrity, it ends up being the people who lead the leaders and, in doing so, avert an almost certain disaster.

President Abraham Lincoln said it best about power. He said that if you really want to see the true character of a person, give them power. Being given power over others will provide the opportunity for which you really are as a person to either shine like the sun or to fall into darkness into the pit of self-destruction and more dangerously, the destruction of others where there may be no escape. Personally, I have been hesitant of being in a leadership position, but will accept leadership if I see the need. On occasion I've sought it out for personal growth purposes, and at other times have actively avoided leadership positions because I did not feel qualified to hold such a position or knew instinctively that I did not have the energy to do the job properly.

I am deathly afraid of being given power. Power is seductive. Power promises prestige, recognition, and control. They are things all of us would like to have. I have seen enough abuses of power, even by people with good intentions, that I fear more the abuses of personal power, especially over others than I desire to wield power. Yet with tongue firmly in-cheek and a nod to J.R.R. Tolkien's *Lord of the Rings* (again!), ever for the "Ring of Power" does that false "Precious" whisper sweet nothings in my ear!

The best leaders lead from a position of strength of character and a high level of knowledge and skill of how to best lead people in order to accomplish a goal. They aren't leaders who just use power to enforce rules, to make themselves look good, or to make or break careers. My style of leadership is tied to the team. For me, we really do sink or swim as a team working for the benefit of all and for the tasks we are given. True power creates and destroys, rarely staying in neutral. It wants to be used, and the more it's used, the happier it is. Power is either a strong-willed, unruly child with no parental oversight and discipline, wreaking havoc wherever it goes or used; or it is used by wise leaders as a disciplined tool, used judiciously, with skill, forethought, and discipline. The proper use of power by those in power can be likened to the scalpel of a highly trained surgeon, used only when needed, and only transformed into the sword of destruction except under the most dire of circumstances.

My prayer for all of us is: "Seek not power for power's sake or leadership for fame or glory. Rather, if given power over others, like young King Solomon, ask God for the wisdom to know how to use it properly for the benefit of others and the welfare of all. Amen.

If you seek a leadership position for personal growth and the desire to be a leader of change for good, then understand that noble birth, nor bloodlines, nor wealth will ensure a successful leadership experience. Even knowledge will not ensure that you will be an effective leader of people, although it is an indispensable tool for good leadership.

I diverge and disagree with Qoheleth's statement, "Woe to you, whose king was a servant". Whether it is because of my Christian faith or even just a lifetime of experience, I have found that it is the leader who willingly becomes the servant of others who make the best leaders. Yes, there are those who having been under the thumb of authority by those who "drank and ate at the wrong times," who, when given leadership authority will repeat those same mistakes under the illusion that it now their time to get their just desserts. The untrained leader and the spiteful leader are a danger to all in their path of authority. Some people believe that there are born leaders and then there are leaders who are trained to be leaders. I personally will take a well-trained leader over the so-called born leader any day of the week. So-called born leaders tend to think of themselves as invincible and/or infallible. History and the passage of time has shined the light on the lie to infallible leaders over and over.

The "servant leader" does not abuse those under them. They seek the general welfare of all those under their authority. They listen to them seriously even when they don't agree with them or must take them on a hard path which they know they would not normally travel. The servant leader tries to ensure that those under them receive the necessary resources in order to succeed. The servant leader will also admit to mistakes and try to learn from them. There is a saying in the military about leadership that goes like: "Praise in public, bitch in private." That means as a leader, you should publicly praise your staff's achievements, and if they screw up, do not publicly admonish them. Rather, in private, help them to correct their mistake. I would rather be a poor servant leader with a clear head and a clear knowledge of my skills and abilities than a king with absolute power but not the wisdom to know how to use it.

"When hands are lazy, the rafters sag; when hands are slack, the house leaks" v. 18. Years ago, when Peg and I were celebrating our twenty-fifth wedding anniversary in Las Vegas, Nevada, at the Hilton Hotel and Casino we went to a Star Trek exhibit. We were walking down the hallway when a young Klingon walked past us and gave us words of wisdom that have stuck with us ever since. He said: "Get off the couch and quit watching TV and go do something with your lives!" We got quite the laugh out of that bit of wisdom, but it really stuck in our heads. So, if your roof is leaking and the rafters are sagging, or if the kitchen sink or toilet is leaking, get off the darn couch and go fix it! If you're like me with two left thumbs for repairing things (and I was a maintenance man for several years in a nursing home; go figure!) then get out your wallet and hire someone to do it for you; don't just sit there getting soaked! As my favorite comic book hero writer Stan Lee used to say: "Nuff said!"

"Bread and oil call forth merriment and wine makes the living glad, but money answers for everything" v. 19. I used to think that only in America does money answer for everything. Qoheleth, however, has set me straight on that erroneous thought by a few thousand years. As a newly retired supervisor from the NYS Education Department after thirty-two-plus years of service, money was constantly on my mind as I got closer and closer to retirement. Then in retirement, money has been on my mind as Peg and I have had to adjust our lifestyle with a reduced and pretty much fixed income. A predicted 6 percent increase in the inflation rate for (2021) didn't calm our anxiety much either.

The need for money throughout the civilized world colors almost everything we do. The need for money influences what we wear, what we eat, and where we live, how we communicate with each other, and how we get our news. It even influences our view of the world around us and the world far from us. Money influences the type and quality of the "bread and oil that calls forth merriment and the wine that makes living glad." There seems to be no escaping the darn need for money. For many of us, it is an eternal struggle between the material needs of life, often only met by having enough money to obtain those things, and the need for a deeply spiritual relationship with God. For those who are believers in God, it is often a constant struggle to balance the two. I must admit it has been a lifetime struggle for me.

God says that for those who love Him, for those who follow in His ways and trust that He will provide us those material things He knows what we need, and they will be provided. In my life and my family's lives, He has indeed provided those things. He has even provided things I don't need from an economic or material needs sense, but which give me pleasure to look at or to indulge in. Yet I would be lying if I said I did not struggle with believing and trusting in His promises. The fears of becoming poor, of not having enough money for at least the basics in life, are real. Ninety percent of the time in our life, those fears and doubts were overblown. The reality did not match the imagined fear. The undue influence of the 10 percent when we were not economically independent makes me angry with myself. Trust is earned, not given, so it has been for me as I've spent a lifetime learning to trust God in all things.

Where is your trust in God, Leon? Where did it fly off to, just because you had to experience a hardship and a temporary one at that? Fear once again enters the picture and clouds that sun of faith.

Is there an answer to that crisis of faith, between the needs of the material world, for money that answers for everything and the desires and needs of the spiritual world? For me, the answer is yes; there is way to overcome the fear and doubt. It has involved *spiritual discipline*. It required the *willful act* of trusting that what God said He would do, He will do. It required me to *activate the faith* that I said I had, by word and deed *on my part*. Sometimes that meant giving a little extra to a charitable cause or giving to a person in need with no expectation that the owed money would be paid back. Sometimes the harder thing to do was to just wait until things unfolded the way they needed to. Hardest yet was to know that I needed the help of others, that I was not the bread winner I saw myself as. For me, humility gave me more wisdom than any success I ever had.

I am now seventy years old, and that struggle between material and spiritual needs has not abated. What I can say is that I continue the struggle. I have not succumbed to a myopic focus on the need for money, and I hope I never will. I have learned to trust God more and more as time marches on, and He has not disappointed me. My prayer for you is that may the good Lord provide you with all the material needs you'll ever need and a few you just want and in doing so you can more fully turn your attention to developing, strengthening, and deepening your relationship of hope, faith, and love with the God of perfect love. Amen.

"Even in your thoughts do not make light of the king, nor in the privacy of your bedroom revile the rich, because the birds of the air may carry your voice, a winged creature may tell what you say" vv. 20. Earlier in this book, I mentioned the actual positives of gossip. I would be remiss if I did not also expound on its evils. Sometimes words have more meaning and a larger impact emotionally and spiritually when presented in song or poem format, for they have a power to cause an emotional response in us that deepens our understanding of the meaning of the words sung, spoken, or written about. In that vein of thought, the following is a sort of hybrid short story and poem about the danger of gossip. May it serve as the requisite warning (physician heal thyself!) about the dangers of a loose tongue.

The Dragoness of Gossip

Ah, the Dragoness of Gossip! She is Queen to the King of Power. Her words are often received with sweetness in the ear, but turn sour in the stomach of our souls when the fruit she bears bursts forth.

Slyly she flies on the dragon wings of rumor. Flitting about from ear to mouth, never satisfied, never satiated until she has spread her lies, and sometimes truths only when it will bear the fruit of destruction and ruin! Daily and nightly she makes her rounds. Her disarming smile is evil, feigning innocence and honest assistance. She only wants to help spread the truth she coyly whispers.

Ever does she seek out the willing, the ignorant, and the eager with dark designs in their hearts. Gossip, lies, and half-truths spew forth from her mouth, dripping like poisoned honey; ever seeking to corrupt the weak-willed and the strong alike. She'll speak the truth openly or in secret if it serves her purpose to sow discord and destruction.

She feeds ever so eagerly on the startled reactions of those who greedily accept her lies, half-truths, and truths; yet she never makes clear which stories are the truth and which ones are lies or even half-truths. Secrets, hidden knowledge, revealed only to you, she promises. She promises secrets to make you powerful, ever so seductively. Power over those who have power over you, she cunningly promises. And the ears that hear and the hearts that accept as gospel truth the lies she spews forth become themselves the spreading virus of gossip. They willingly spread their disease across the land, never understanding that viruses never build up, never create; they only consume and destroy the sender and the receiver until only death is left in its wake.

She leaves our thoughts in doubt, anger, fear, and frustration. She eagerly watches for the effect her gossip has on the person hearing it. If it has a positive effect, it is only by accident. Her gossips are the rotting eggs of disruption and discord, and she readily and eagerly gives birth to them. They in turn wreck their own havoc on the world as they spread the evil web of gossip ever wider, ever deeper into the dark recesses of human souls.

Finally, when she has just enough gossip to influence those in power, she returns to her cavern of darkness and doubt and silently whispers into the ear of the ultimate King Dragon of Power her lies, her half-truths, and truths. The King of Power is not immune to her soft, evil whispers, for the King will do anything and accept any rumor in order to keep his most precious jewel: power. She clarifies nothing for the Dragon King of Power. She does not tell him what to do with the information she has given him, for she fears the power he has to destroy her with the light of truth if he can but see past her lies. She only seeks to disturb him enough to light the fires of his wrath and his desire to retain power at all costs. Her eyes of hell's fire burn hotly with delight as he is aroused to bring his power to bear on those who will bear the brunt of his actions, of those whom he perceives would dare usurp his power.

Innocence or guilt matters not to the Queen Dragoness of Gossip, nor to the King of Power. She only delights in her King's ability to wield power for ruin or rise. He delights in his ability to wield power. And in his singular desire to retain all power to himself, he in wrath, wields that power over others in full force to destroy or to create, for ruin or rise of the innocent and guilty alike. The Dragoness of Gossip smiles approvingly and quietly turns once more to silently slither out into a world of willing ears and loose lips eager for power, fame, and prestige regardless of the cost to self or others so as to stir once again the wrath of the King Dragon of Power to the destruction, ruin, or rise of many.

May the Spirit of God within you enable you to know when to shut your ears and close your mouths and guard your hearts and minds to her evil influence so that you may keep your dignity and integrity intact before the Lord God of heaven and earth. Amen!

Chapter 11

"Cast your bread upon the waters; after a long time you may find it again. Make seven or eight portions; you know not what misfortune may come upon the earth" vv. 1–2. My Bible interprets the first sentence as possibly referring to the spirit of adventure in business and/or to generosity in almsgiving. Waters may refer to the ocean and how much trade, profit and loss, the ancients experienced as part of their business deals plying the Mediterranean trade routes. The second sentence seems to imply not trusting by putting at risk your wealth into only one business enterprise. It may also refer to giving to multiple charities (i.e., almsgiving) as perhaps an outward sign to God for a blessing in return for a person's entrepreneurial efforts. I personally interpret it as "saving for a rainy day" emergency situation. The rainy day may be for a business need that must be met but wasn't anticipated. It may be just saving for a day when one's income is unexpectedly cut short, such as a job loss or a business failure.

Both ideas are good business and spiritual ideas. Life's unexpected twists and turns teach us soon enough that unexpected things will happen in our lifetimes. Some such turns, despite the chaos they bring, can be a good turn of events that lead us to love, wealth, and wisdom. Others can lead to disaster; it's one of the reasons insurance of all kinds exist. I've carried life insurance almost my entire adult life. Peg and I even took out life insurance on our children. Life's unexpected turns also teaches us to save up money for those rainy-day situations.

Entrepreneurs have always had that spirit of adventure in business. I've always admired their ability to risk their own wealth, time, and effort in order to succeed in their material life and perhaps in the higher level of social status that a successful business enterprise might bring. When I was in my thirties, I tried my hand a being an entrepreneur. I cast my bread upon the waters, and the bread (i.e., effort) pretty much sank to the bottom! I tried coming up with an idea of selling information before Google ever existed. Unfortunately, technology back in the 1970s didn't match my vision. It was pretty much the idea of just sending people to the right sources of information, mostly dealing with government information (libraries anyone?). That idea died on the vine pretty quickly.

My second effort was a little more successful but not by a whole lot. I became a "Face Painter." I even wrote a small book that I had copyrighted on how to drum up business. I also provided ideas for subjects to paint. I gave myself the name of "Mr. Doodle-O!" It was not a "get-rich-scheme." It was a way to make a little money on the side of a person's main job. I managed to even get advertised on a local radio station in Syracuse, New York, when a local mall hired me to paint children's faces.

While that entrepreneurial effort didn't go far it did help me land a good job with the NYS Education Department in Albany, New York. I had taken a state civil service exam and passed it. It provided an opportunity for a job interview. During the interview, I was asked about my experiences, and I related my Mr. Doodle-O experience. The person who interviewed me also had a couple of side business efforts. He appreciated my effort, as minor as it was, and ended offering me the job right on the spot. It turned into a thirty-two-plus-year career with eventual promotions along the way. My entrepreneurial bread upon the waters as a face painter didn't pan out, but it went along a current that I did not envision and came back to me with a career. How's that for casting one's bread upon the waters?

How does one cast their spiritual bread upon the waters and what spiritual portions can we make in preparation for a day of misfortune? What might be some types of spiritual bread?

The first spiritual bread we might consider is adopting the *spirit of adventure* that entrepreneurs have when they attempt to engage in a successful business enterprise. Many people view spiritual people as "staid-in-the-wool," boringly consistent, and definitely not adventurous. The word *sheep* often comes to mind for many people. They often view spiritual people as people who use God as a crutch and as a shield against life's hardships and misfortunes. For truly, deeply spiritual people, nothing could be further from the truth.

So what do entrepreneurs and spiritual people have in common? They both have *faith*. The business person has faith that their ideas, their material resources, business connections, and their own personal efforts will lead to success in business. Like those of us who proclaim a belief and a faith in God, business people do not actually know that they will succeed. Their efforts at success are based on their faith that what they do will succeed.

Spiritual people must, in faith and hope, toss their spiritual bread upon the waters of faith in the hope that those waters will bring them back their spiritual bread multiplied sevenfold and then some. Spiritual people no more *know* what the final outcome of their spiritual adventure upon the living waters of faith will bring than the business entrepreneur *knows* the final outcome of all their efforts at trying to succeed in business. Both travel in hope and faith. One seeks a material gain; the other seeks something more elusive— the presence of the divine in their lives. Material gain in business can, in a sideways manner, lead potentially to spiritual gain. Many a grateful heart has turned to God in thanksgiving. Many a successful person has shared their gained wealth with others. It is not, however, a direct route to the divine presence of God in their lives. Often the material gain route simply leads to either more material gain or ruin when the only reality seen by the business person is material wealth.

A spiritual person is a spiritual entrepreneur. They are adventurers of the unknown. They travel in faith and hope. Sometimes the spiritual path to a deeper relationship with the divine is clearly marked out. Spiritual guideposts are clearly marked out along the way. For most of us, however, the path is not clear; no specific guideposts of accomplishment are provided until the spiritual adventurer actually reaches the guidepost. Eventually the spiritual entrepreneur begins to realize that the journey of faith itself is a journey in and with the divine Presence. The divine Presence they were seeking was actually with them the entire time!

What type of spiritual bread does a person of faith toss upon the waters? What resources do they need for the journey? Is there a guide for how many portions we set aside for those days of misfortune? We've already mentioned the spiritual bread and waters of faith and hope. The third piece needed is the spiritual bread of love. Love feeds us along our spiritual journey. It nourishes our hearts, minds, and souls. Through love of self, family, and friends, and most importantly love of God, we are able to travel the waters of faith with confidence that whatever spiritual bread we cast upon the waters of faith will come back to us at the proper time and place and with the needed spiritual gifts in order to help us deepen God's divine presence within us.

All journeys need resources to assist the journeyman along the way. The spiritual journey is no different. So what are some of those spiritual resources? Listed below are some but not all spiritual resources available to us that strengthen us along our way.

- Prayer—either formal or informal as a direct interaction and communication with God. It can be said in a formal religious service or as an individual petition. Daily and nightly prayers are for me a constant strengthener of my spiritual breads of hope, faith, and love in God.

- Religion—for me personally, the definition of religion is a group of people who come together as community to worship God with all their hearts, minds, and souls; who seek to love their neighbors as they love themselves, who seek to properly do His will here on Earth, and something I've added over the years because of its importance, to be good stewards of this beautiful planet that God has given to us to live out our days on. As a born Roman Catholic, the tenets of Catholicism guide my religious observances. I went searching for more formal definitions of religion, but there seemed to be so many that I leave it up to you, the reader, to search for your own meaning of religion that makes the most sense to you.

- Rituals/Sacraments; All religions have rituals or sacraments of some type. The rituals themselves will not necessarily bring a person closer to God, but they can assist a person in focusing their hearts and minds properly on God. It is an individual's attitude, belief, and love of and in God that gives force and strength to a ritual or a sacrament. A community of believers and lovers of God strengthen that faith, hope, and love even more. A ritual or sacrament without the proper religious attitude toward God is devoid of purpose and force. As a baptized Roman Catholic the highest form of and most meaningful sacrament for me is the reception of the Holy Eucharist, the body and blood of our Lord Jesus Christ. The host and cup are more than symbols for me. They are the literal body and blood of Jesus Christ the Son of God in the form of bread and wine. But even that belief would be an empty ritual/sacrament, devoid of meaning and purpose, if I did not believe in the reality of God and of His love for me.

- Practicing what you preach—practicing one's faith is a daily exercise. Words alone never make faith a reality. If we daily practice making a reality to our hope, faith, and love of God and our neighbors, then our spiritual bread upon the waters and the souls it will nurture will be multiplied beyond count.

My prayer for all of us is that no matter what formal or informal religion you adhere to, may its rituals and sacraments be made fruitful and meaningful to you and your community of worshippers because of your hope, faith, and love of God, and your ready acceptance of His love for you. Amen.
"When the clouds are full, they pour rain upon the earth. Whether a tree falls to the south or to the north, wherever it falls there it shall be. One who pays heed to the wind will not sow, and one who watches the clouds will never reap" vv. 3–4. "Que Sera, Sera—Whatever will be, will be" so goes the famous Italian phrase in a song written by the team of Jay Livingston and Ray Evans back in 1955 and made famous by actress Doris Day in the Alfred Hitchcock film, *The Man Who knew Too Much*. There are

two parts to Qoheleth's statements above. The first is the belief that in life, no matter what choices you make, you will not always know the outcome of your choices and that despite trying to be the captain of your own ship, what will be, will be. It's fate; it's destiny, it's in the cards. It's not an excuse to not make any decisions; it's just an acknowledgment that you'll have no control over some things in life. Accepting that fact can actually help you move on in life and not be stuck in an experience that might paralyze you from taking necessary future actions. Some people might see the sentence as fatalistic and use it as an excuse to do nothing since everything is already ordained. God will never accept that excuse from us for lack of effort on our part. In an odd way, God tells us that free will is our destiny, and free will is the determining factor in where the tree of faith with its deep roots falls in the forest of our lives.

The second sentence has been my personal boogeyman of not accomplishing things in my life because I'm too busy paying heed to the wind and watching the clouds go by. Full admittance here; I love life. In fact, I kind of love it too much. Everything about life distracts me. I love observing the weather, people, learning new things, useful or useless. No sooner has my attention been caught by the latest news or discovery, than something else catches my eye and imagination. I compensate for this bugaboo characteristic of mine by doing many little things over the course of my life. I'll write a little here, draw or paint something there, but the big thing would always elude me; or, to be honest, I'd let something else district me from the big thing. My recognition that it was commitment and all the energy and effort that must go into any major endeavor that kept me from doing that one big thing. It was and has been more fun and less work to get lost in the castle of my imagination. If, as noted in the New Testament by Jesus, I cleaned house of the one demon of distraction and did not commit to keeping the house clean of other useless distractions, then seven more demons of distraction would enter and take up residence. *And I didn't seem to mind.* Ouch and double ouch on calling myself to task on my own laziness!

It wasn't until I retired and I've been able to take about eight months to reflect on my past life through prayer, meditation, and reading forty-one years of journals, and writing in my spiritual journal; that the spiritual light bulb of inspiration lit up, and I saw the one thing that I had committed to during my life. It was my relationship to God and a desire to deepen and strengthen that relationship. Journal after journal entry over the years showed me myself and that desire to increase God's divine presence in my life. Thus was born the seed for the creation of this book. I have tried writing other books, but none were ever finished. This book you are reading now is my big accomplishment. It may be a short book, but it is a completed book. For me, it was God who cleared away the distractions and allowed me to commit to this endeavor, to clear out the many demons of distractions, pleasant as they might be, and keep my spiritual house clean of them so I can focus on what is really important to me: God.

Please understand this; those demons of distraction have not disappeared. They are constantly knocking on the doors and windows of my imagination. If a crack forms, they'll be inside in an instant. My sword and my shield against them is God and my commitment to deepen my relationship with Him. God's love for me and my love for Him and my desire to express that love in thought, word, and deed have so far enabled me to continue the constant struggling to put my spiritual imagination in Him and only Him.

Within the phrase: "One who pays heed to the wind will not sow, and one who watches the clouds will never reap," there is also the implication that an obsessive desire to wait until the right time to act can actually stop you from succeeding in something you'd like to accomplish. Timing is everything, people say, but time is not endless for us in this life. Time has an end date for all of us. Waiting for the right time to act is wisdom, but sometimes life doesn't give us a right time to act, only time to act. It is wisdom to know that you may need to heed the wind while sowing, and to reap while watching the wind of fortune blow wherever it may.

My prayer for us all who seek communion with God is that whatever demons of distraction impede our relationship with Him that He may through His grace and love remove them from us and in doing so, we become creatures of commitment and creation and not just observers of it. Amen.

"Just as you know not how the breath of life fashions the human frame in the mother's womb, so you know not the work of God which He is accomplishing in the universe" v. 5.

Rather than a discourse on the meaning of Qoheleth's words I would rather like to offer up a prayer that speaks to God and the work that He is accomplishing in the universe:

Dear God in heaven,
The minds of men have explored and discovered how the breath of life fashions the human frame in the mother's womb. That discovery has not diminished the wonderful mystery of life itself. If anything, it has increased our awe and wonder of You and Your divine, creative works. Where

some see but a natural process, others see the loving creative hand of God.

Science, too, has opened up humanity's eyes to the heavens above. Uncountable galaxies and stars stretch out to infinity. Diamonds of light fill our imaginations. Worlds are now newly discovered, yet the breath of life not yet found in them. Are we the only ones in this vast universe You created? Are there others You created for the sake of Your love? Though we see the heavens in all of its glorious beauty, still we know not the work which you are accomplishing in the universe.

Again science has been able to roughly calculate the age of our known universe: 14 billion years since You first formed it with but a spoken word. What wonders of creation long lost must you have created? Were there other sons and daughters of God before us? Did they rise and fall as cosmic dust in a celestial wind? Did you give them souls also? Are they now reunited with you or have they gone into permanent death and oblivion? Will we meet brothers and sisters and children of God as we reach out into the galaxy? Will we find out that we are all children of God or that there are in fact only a few "chosen ones"?

You are the Alpha and the Omega; what are we in heaven's design? Your ways are indeed a mystery, oh Lord! You have made our lives but a passing shadow, a small burst of light quickly gone in an expanding universe that has no end, on a celestial timeline that no clock will ever be able to record. For what ultimate purpose do we exist in such an expansive universe whose timeline is measured in billions of years, but whose human life is not even measured as a blink in Your eyes?

Dear Lord, whatever the work You are accomplishing in the universe with Your hands, somewhere in those loving hands may we reside as one of Your greatest accomplishments of love and creation. Amen.

Qoheleth Continues:

vv. 6 "In the morning sow your seed, and at evening let your hand not be idle: for you know not which of the two will be successful, or whether both will turn out well." In my Bible I have a small hand-written note that states: "Have a backup plan!" To be honest, once I got my job with the NYS Education Department, I had no back-up plan that ever came to fruition. I tried painting as a side job. I tried writing fantasy/science fiction books and maybe sold a couple of pieces of artwork. However, life, being the sneaky thing it is, got in the way of trying not to have an idle hand at nighttime. As parents of three children and long workdays, we were too tired by evening time to even consider doing something extra. Even with a good NYS civil service job, it would be at least a decade and a half before my salary and Peg's salary started to push ahead of the middle-class curve.

The wisdom in Qoheleth's words should be apparent to everyone with at least a little common sense. Two incomes are better than one, and three or four incomes are even better. Implementing that common-sense strategy is a lot harder to do when you've just got enough energy to provide for a little more than the basic necessities of life. I suppose if I were to give any advice on the subject, it might go a little contrary to Qoheleth's advice. Working for material wealth can only bring a person so much happiness. Money can buy fun experiences, Disneyland for example. Working can pay for some pleasures only money can buy.

I have found the dogged pursuit of money and material wealth to be personally unfulfilling. I traded in the time I could have used to not have idle hands in the evening, trying to earn extra income for time with my family and friends, for time with my neighbors, and time volunteering with my church community and the Boy Scouts of America (BSA). My two sons are BSA Eagle Scouts because I diverted my time and attention to them rather than the pursuit of material comfort and wealth. I would often complain (perhaps whine would be more accurate) about the lack of funds, but I can honestly say that for me personally, the tradeoff for the time I had with those I loved left me with no regrets. Money could not buy the beautiful memories and experiences with family and friends I hold deeply within my heart. Trading that time for acts of love actually helped me to trust and have faith that God would take care of those material and physical needs so I could more fully take care of my personal needs of the heart and soul. Since I'm not in the proverbial poorhouse at the moment, I'd say that faith in God has shown itself to be true.

Whatever path you choose to take in how you use your free time if I were to give one last piece of guidance it would be this: If your heart, mind, and soul are in unified agreement on a particular course of action, then you're most likely going in the right direction. May the God of heaven and earth guide us all to such a wonderful alignment of heart, mind, and soul. Amen.

Poem on Youth and Old Age:

> Light is sweet! And it is pleasant for the eyes to see the sun. However many years a man may live, let him, as he enjoys them all, remember that the days of darkness will be many. All that is to come is vanity.
>
> > *Rejoice, O young man, while you are young, and let your heart be glad in the days of your youth.* Follow the ways of your heart, the vision of your eyes; yet understand that as regards all this, God will bring you to judgement. Ward off grief from your heart and put away trouble from your presence, though the dawn of youth is fleeting. vv. 7–10

May I humbly add: "Rejoice young and old, rejoice sons and daughters, rejoice one and all, for the life God has given you, for the life you've already lived and the life yet to be lived. May God's blessings allow you to follow the ways of your heart, mind, and soul. May we all humbly remember that all that we do for good or ill, seen or unseen by men, will be judged by the most high God of heaven and earth; for some things while we still draw breath under the sun, for others at the final judgment where a life of eternal light or darkness will await us. May you, to the best of your ability and with the love of God within your heart and in the presence and company of close family and friends, banish grief from your heart. May trouble be only as close as the farthest star in the universe. May you with the fullness of your heart enjoy the dawn of youth, which is indeed fleeting; may it be turned into a middle-age of honor and accomplishment, and may your old age be the golden age and pinnacle of your wisdom, hope, faith, and love of God for all to see so that your life is more than a shadow and a vanity under the sun. Amen.

Chapter 12

Remember your Creator in the days of your youth,
before the evil days come and the years approach of which
you will say,
I have no pleasure in them; before the sun is darkened, and
the light, and the moon, and the stars, while the clouds return
after the rain;
When the guardians of the house tremble, and the strong men
are bent, and the grinders are idle because they are few, and
they who look through the windows grow blind;
When the doors to the street are shut, and the sound of the
mill is low; When one waits for the chirp of a bird, and all the
daughters of song are suppressed; and one fears heights, and
perils in the street;
When the almond tree blooms, and the locust grow sluggish
and the caper berry is without effect, because man goes to his
lasting home, and mourners go about the streets; before the
silver cord is snapped and the golden bowl broken, and the
pitcher is shattered in the spring, and the broken pulley falls
into the well, and dust returns to earth as it once was, ***and the***
life breath returns to God who gave it.

Vanity of vanities, says Qoheleth, all things are vanity. vv. 1–8

FOR ME, AS I've read this poem of Qoheleth over and over, I find no room for improvement; no words to enhance it. It does two very important things for me. Within the brevity of my life, the poem does make me remember my Creator. I think about the many blessings He has provided our family through the years.

And in a contrast of thoughts and emotions, it not only makes me contemplate the brevity of life and the hard times that often come with life, but it also helps me to remember the good things in life. I remember that I take great pleasure in the light of the sun and the light of the moon and the stars. I remember the delight I take in a gentle rain and the breaking of the sun through the clouds after the rain, and the joy of seeing a rainbow burst forth in all its wondrous colors; sometime even being delighted as the sky yields a second or third rainbow on top of the first. I contemplate the deep and moving memories imbedded in the very walls of our home, as we raised a family, with all of its trials and tribulations. Just this morning, I took the innocent delight of looking out our dining room bay window and watching an early morning sun breaking through the clouds after a heavy night of rainfall. I remember over the unfolding years of my life the many open doors of friendship and love inviting me in.

I remember with fondness a lifetime of work that gave me an income, but more importantly skills, challenges, and friendships. I recall the chirping and whistling of birds of many different kinds, bringing nature's music to my ears. I remember trusting in God in those instances where I faced fears with courage and with hope because I believed He was with me in those times of trial and tribulation. I recall that how, in trusting God to be with me, those hard times helped mold me, taught me patience and the power of perseverance. I remember the smell of spring flowers playing tippy toe with my nose! I remember, and still feel the touch of wet sand between my toes on an endless stretch of beach, the lapping of ocean waves over my feet and ankles, and the smell of salt air. My mind and body remembers plunging into cold waters of lakes, rivers, and ponds. There can never be too many sunrises and sunsets. Even now before autumn and winter sets in, I take joy in the beauty of wild and garden flowers and in so doing come to revere the preciousness of life.

Now at the age of seventy, the poem cannot but help me meditate on the day of my death: "before the silver cord is snapped and the golden bowl broken, and the pitcher is shattered in the spring, and the broken pulley falls into the well, and dust returns to earth as it once was, and the (*my*) life breath returns to God who gave it."

All of these things Qoheleth's poem makes me ponder and ruminate; from the gift of life itself, to hard times not only endured, but from which, with God's grace and loving embrace, my family and I have thrived; to my inevitable death. In addition, the phrase: "*and the life breath returns to God who gave it*" gives me hope that death is not the final outcome of our short lives; instead we return to Him who created us out of the desire to love us and be loved by us.

In that contemplation I do not see my life as vanity of vanities. Rather, I see my life as a passing spring flower, a shooting star across the night sky that catches the eyes of God, and in my brief moment of life, I enable Him to smile and take joy in the realization that it was He who created this brief thing of beauty that was me.

Qoheleth's Epilogue

> Besides being wise, Qoheleth taught the people knowledge, and weighed, scrutinized and arranged many proverbs. Qoheleth sought to find pleasing sayings, and to write down true sayings with precision. The sayings of the wise are like goads; like fixed spikes are the topics given by one collector. As to more than these, my son, beware. Of the making of many books there is no end, and in much study there is weariness for the flesh. The last word, when all is heard; fear God and keep His commandments, for this is man's all; because God will bring to judgement every work, with all its hidden qualities, whether good or bad. vv. 9–13

My Bible's footnote points out the spiritual meaning behind the words *goads* and *collector*. It states that the sayings (proverbs/topics) were to be stimulants to thought. I assume it meant religious and spiritual thought. Ecclesiastes certainly has done that for me. The footnote goes on to say that the meaning of "fixed spikes" is specific topics around which spiritual and religious contemplation and thought would be centered.

To a large extent the purpose behind this book is to create fuel for thought, meditation, contemplation, and prayer on God, on His acts of creation and on the miracle of His creation: you! I want, through the words of Qoheleth and my interpretation of them, to have all of us contemplate the shortness of life, of how the work we do will not last into eternity, but unlike Qoheleth, not despair over such thoughts. Rather I hope through some of my words to convince you that such a God of creation, mercy, and love would not create us with souls that can directly connect to Him in hope, faith, and love, only to go into a permanent death, an everlasting darkness. Such a God of love and creation has made those whom He calls His own to never be forgotten, to outlast the stars in the night sky, made to reside in the Holy Spirit of God for all eternity.

Chapter 12

With sincere apologies to Qoheleth, it appears that with this book I have just added to the never-ending pile of making books! Hopefully, he will forgive my indulgence at a humble attempt at trying to find true and pleasing sayings with some precision at least and to honor the sage or sages who wrote the beautiful words of Ecclesiastes. I also do agree with Qoheleth that too much studying can be wearying to the flesh. I have a handwritten note next to the saying that says: "Of books, yes, of *learning*, I hope and pray no!" I also wrote a short interpretation statement about endless studying. I wrote: "i.e., go out and live a little!" Qoheleth and the shortness of our lives have altered my interpretation somewhat over the years. I think maybe we need to go out and live a lot!

I am not in total agreement with Qoheleth's last sentence. I agree with everything he wrote. I agree that we should reverently fear God, understanding that we will be judged by Him. I agree that all our works, both good and bad, will be judged by Him. I agree that it is important to keep His commandments. They are the building blocks and spiritual foundation to a just and peaceful person and society. Keeping God's commandments takes our lives beyond mere survival. They allow us to use our minds, our hearts, and spirits for acts of creation and for spreading justice, peace, and love to all that we come in contact with.

Where I come to disagreement with Qoheleth is his statement: "for this is man's all." If you, the reader, should come away with one important thought and belief of mine that I hope is apparent throughout this short book, it is this: our purpose in life, whether you believe in life after death, or don't believe it, but believe in the reality of God is to love the Lord our God with all are hearts, minds, and souls; and allow Him to love you with His whole being. I also believe that the more sincere your effort, the more successful your effort to love God will be, and if you love Him with your whole being, the less you will have to fear Him, and the more you will be able to embrace the fullness of the life He has given you.

When I was a child, I respected my father and mother and feared them. The fear, however, was limited to going against their will by knowingly doing something I knew was wrong before I even did it. The fear and respect that

I had for them and their power over me as a child did not diminish my love for them. My love for them and their love for me dominated my relationship with them, not my fear of them. So it is in my relationship to God. The more I sincerely try to love Him, the more I sincerely try to serve Him and follow His commandments, the less I fear Him because I'm too busy loving Him and happily accepting His love for me.

My final thoughts and prayers on the final chapter to Ecclesiastes for everyone is that: "The last word, when all is heard; fear God and keep His commandments, *love God with all your heart, mind, and soul, and your neighbor as yourself, for this is man's all*; because God will bring to judgement every work, every heart, false or true, with all their hidden qualities, whether good or bad." Amen.

Chapter 13

Final Thoughts: My Personal Moment of Ecclesiastes

Ecclesiastes has always had a place in my heart and spiritual imagination. I, in fact, wrote my own little Qoheleth poem about being remembered or forgotten. For despite my faith in God and the promise of an afterlife, I sometimes sink into moments of despair and pessimism that my life mattered, that it had some type of positive and lasting impact that would remain after I died. Most of us wonder if we had some type of lasting impact in life because we existed. This unique, precious life of ours gives us so many moments of joy and sadness that we cannot but help wonder to what purpose it was all for if we go to our grave and to either an eternal darkness or an eternal nothingness so that even we won't know that we existed.

It's one of the reasons back in 1980, when someone gave me a drawing journal that I started to draw and to write my thoughts down on my life as it progressed through the years. Those journals are not great works of art. They are not master literary pieces to be enshrined in some literary hall of fame for all to see and to last for centuries after my passing. They are for the here and now and for my children and grandchildren, and maybe even great-grandchildren. They are documented family history, and their importance became more apparent to me when back in the spring of 2004 my youngest son Michael got a journaling assignment from his English junior high school class at North Colonie, Central School District. I wrote him a personal note about how important the assignment was in providing him a means to tell the world a little something about himself that he might think was important for other people to know. Life for him, as it does for many young people, got busy, and he did not carry the tradition forward. Perhaps his wonderful wife Taylor reading this may start their own tradition of journaling. But down the road of life when he has more time to reflect, he may remember what I wrote to him and carry the mantle of journaling forward.

I believe my daughter Theresa has carried it forward to an extent, though I'm not sure how often she gets to write now that she's an entrepreneur making and managing her own handmade soaps and lotions, and selling them in her store, T & J Handcrafted Soap, in Troy, New York. She has always been very good at documenting (and expressing) her feelings—all of them!

My oldest son Larry is so busy being a father to two precocious daughters, Madeline and Lorelei, a husband to his beautiful wife Erin, and a senior communications director at Mack Molding Company, Northern Division in Vermont, that journaling is probably very far from his mind. So it's left up to Dad and Mom who in recent years have joined me on my journaling adventure. Peg and I know that sooner or later as time allows, they will all want to remember their lives in a more tangible way than just memory itself. That is the gift we will be leaving behind for them.

Perhaps to help stimulate your desire to be remembered through journaling, I present to you below my letter to Michael as he was about to start his journaling assignment. It is slightly edited for better clarity, and was written in the love of a father for his son. May it stir something in you to leave a little something of yourself to history and to a generation you will never know until they meet you on the other side of life, and they get to tell you how what you left behind had an impact on their lives so that you will not feel as Qoheleth did that your life is not but a "vanity of vanities, a chase after wind."

Foreword to Michael Q. Hovish from His Dad on a Shaker Junior High School Journaling Assignment—May 2004

History is not only the recording of great events that shape and mold the lives of peoples and nations. History is also the making and recording of the everyday events of our own lives. Through the writing project you are about to be immersed in, you will begin, through words, to weave the fabric of your everyday life into a garment of unique beauty. It will be a reflection of you to the world. It will in a small but significant way become an actual part of history. In all works of creation, whether it be another life, a book, or a work of art, the first mental step you must take is to be honest with yourself and to the audience you wish to share your creation with. Without honesty, the foundation of your written words will be built upon the proverbial house of sand. When the harsh winds of reality and truth blow, the foundation will crumble, and your audience will disappear and by extension so will your creation. You do not have to be harsh or cruel with yourself; you can be gentle. But above all else, you must be truthful to the words that will flow from your pen, from your heart and soul, for you are worth telling the truth about.

You are going to do something that I wish members of my own family had done years ago: write and document their dreams and beliefs and about the events in their everyday lives that have helped shape and mold the person they became. From my grandfather Joseph Hovish who came to these shores in 1900 from Poland, to your mom's relatives who have been here since the Revolutionary War, there are countless stories lost, untold and unknown. Many of our grandparents and great-grandparents' generations went about the business of building this country and raising families without particular thought about passing on who they were to the next generation, just as long as there was another generation. But they never realized the hunger they would leave behind in their children to know from whence and whom they came. The leaves on the family tree want to look back at the roots from which they came. They want to know their family history and how it shaped their identity.

You are about to take an important step in that direction, not only for yourself, but also as a precious gift to those who love you now and will love you in the future. Do not underestimate the power of your words to move another just because you are young. The zeal with which you live your life now will be transmitted into the words you write. Your very essence, if you remain faithful to the truth, will reveal itself in your written words. And who knows, someday a son, a daughter, a wife, or dear friend will read those words, and they will give strength to their own identity and a sense of connectedness to generations past and future.

You are our favorite youngest son! Enjoy yourself on this journey of exploration into who you are in the world. You have so much to offer; a neat sense of humor, musical talent, a great singing voice, loyalty to your friends, and a keen inquiring mind. Through your words let the world know just who Michael Q. Hovish was during the past year and who he might become in the years ahead. And we hope that you will take this opportunity to not only begin, but also to continue the journey of self-exploration through writing and documenting the events of your life, even after this assignment is done.

The following poem was written as an addition to my son Michael on his journaling assignment. It is slightly changed from the original version to better reflect how I've come to view God in my life and life itself as the years passed by. I've come to view it over the years as my own personal Qoheleth poem on the vanity of life. I hope you enjoy it.

Will I Be Remembered?
By Leon W. Hovish
May 2004 and Revised November 2021

My soul soars to heights unknown,
Through art, dance, and song, and now through words,
The contents of my heart revealed, laid bare for all to see.
My dreams unfold in marvelous ways,
And my laughter and tears, born of sorrow and joy rain down upon the landscape of my life; revealed in these words.
As my life's footsteps have walked along the sandy beaches of time, time's passing seems to wash away the memory of my life's footsteps. Who will remember my life; full of experiences great and small, wondrous and painful? Who will know or remember the lush and barren lands I have trod; of my loving many, hating few; will no traces of me be found by those who follow after me?
Will the winds of eternity blow away the footprints of my life on those sandy beaches of time?

Chapter 13

Who will know of this Life I've lived and of my Loves lost and found,
and created?
Who will know of a heart wounded, and healed by the loving touch
of another?
Who will see how God has touched my soul and in doing so changed my
life forever?
Who will know from whence I came or wither I go?
If I do not leave some trace of myself behind,
Will mankind ever know I existed?
My soul cries out . . .
I lived! I loved! And I existed!
And I existed . . .
I existed . . .
I . . .
. . .

The three dots at the end of the poem signify the idea that my existence, the memory and knowledge of me has faded to nothingness. So Qoheleth and I have more in common on the vanity of a human life that I'd like to admit. Yet hope in God and His promise of eternal life with Him springs eternal in our human souls. It springs eternal in me.

In the autumn of September 2018, I once again visited the idea behind Qoheleth's lament. I composed a prayer to my children, grandchildren, and all those who would follow until our family name would be no more. It is a prayer of hope born of the love of God that leads to faith and continues our ability to love and hope even in times of darkness and adversity. May it provide some consolation and stir in your soul the belief that God did not make our souls a temporary thing to be brought down to oblivion and eternal darkness at our passing away in this life. Rather, may this prayer stir in your soul the inspiration that fuels your faith that God made you for His eternal love, a love that will outlast the stars and the galaxies.

What Mankind Forgets, God Will Remember

May God want to remember you by the life you've led.

Just as you do, God will remember who you loved and how deeply and purely you loved.

He will remember how you followed through on the prayer, meditation, and application of His holy and living Word in your life, as revealed through the Holy Scriptures.

He will remember who and what you hated or loved and the thoughts and actions that flowed from your hatred and love. If you must hate something, hate evil in all its forms and manners. Love all that is good in this world.

Remember, the defeat of evil comes not from fighting fire with fire, that is, to return evil for evil, but to return evil with love, as best you can. When you can't, and there will come a time when you can't, ask for the grace of God to do so.

I have learned, and I hope you do too, that there are some things too big, so overwhelming in our lives, that we cannot overcome them by our own efforts. Healing and salvation in those moments of despair and loss must come through reliance upon our loving God and the others He sends into our lives to help us. It is a strange and humbling thing to rely on something or someone you cannot see but can only feel. Yet, it is possible, as all things are possible with God, who loves you dearly.

Reliance upon God to travel with us in life and to assist us when needed, especially during the dark times, is not to see God as a crutch or an excuse or as a mystical placebo, or as a "Short-Order Cook of Miracles!" It is to see Him as He truly is, the Creator, the Defender, the Lover, the Forgiver, and the source of all good blessings, the Healer and the Consoler. You cannot see Him directly, but if you love Him, have faith and hope in Him, you will feel Him—always!

To the best of your ability, train your spiritual ears to hear His Word and commit your heart to do His will. I must confess at the age of sixty-nine, I have not mastered that skill. It appears to be a lifelong job and commitment, and there appears to be no perfect moments when you will attain perfection

Chapter 13

in hearing His Word and fulfilling His will at all times. But I won't stop trying to hear Him better, follow His Word, and commit to His will better, nor should you.

Finally, the harsh reality, and the reason I started writing this "prayer." In the end, with the endless passage of time, you will be forgotten. You will exist on this earth as long as the last person to remember you lives. The wind and the dust will sweep over your grave, your headstone will crumble, your ashes, whether scattered or interned in one place, will disappear, and even mankind will disappear. When finally, all is silent nothingness, and even the stars blink out of sight, there will only be God to remember you. My final question and prayer for you then is:

What will God eternally remember about you that He should take you into eternity with Him?

In Closing:

To all my family, friends, neighbors, and strangers who took the time to read this book of mine; thank you for taking the time to read it. I hope you can see the honesty and love with which this book was written. You have given me the gift of great joy today for letting me share myself with you.

May God bless you and keep you ever in His mind, heart, and Holy Spirit. May He take great joy in your being, in your creation, so that you may abide with Him for all eternity, never to be forgotten, never to exist as a vanity of vanities or a chase after wind.

Amen.

Photograph and Illustration Credits

Cover Page—NASA Hubble Space Telescope—NGC 7293
Page 3—The New American Bible—Photo by Leon Hovish
Page 5—The Sun—NASA James Webb Space Telescope
Page 9—Spiral Galaxy—NASA Hubble Space Telescope
Page 12—Self portrait of Author Leon Hovish as Santa Claus
Page 13—Stonehenge England—Photo Taken by Leon Hovish—2011
Page 25—Yosemite National Park—El Capitan—Photo Taken by Leon Hovish—2015
Page 26—Photo of Peggy Hovish and Grandchildren Madeline and Lorelei Hovish—Christmas 2020—Photo Taken by Leon Hovish
Page 31—Photo of Casket Taken by Leon Hovish 2012
Page 35—Photo of Money Cross Taken by Leon Hovish
Page 63—Photo of Peggy and Leon Hovish—Photo Taken by Theresa (Hovish) Van Duyne 2011
Page 64—View of Earth from the Moon—NASA Photo—NASA50_52-_02_ON08
Page 69—Photo of Madeline Hovish and Quincy Taken by Leon Hovish—2017
Page 92—NASA Hubble Space Telescope—Vastness of Space—Hubble_g035_2
Page 95—Hovish Family Cemetery Plot—Photo Taken by Leon Hovish—2012
Page 98—Christ Our Light Roman Catholic Church, Loudonville NY—Altar Area with Reflection of Mary—Photo Taken by Leon Hovish
Page 105—Self-Portrait of the Author Leon W. Hovish—December 2020

About the Author

Leon Walter Hovish is a recently retired New York State (NYS) government supervisor of educational programs within the Office of Every Student Succeeds Act (ESSA) Programs of the NYS Education Department, after having served over thirty-two years with the Department. Leon is also a thirteen-year veteran, having served three years in the US Marine Corps during the Vietnam Era from 1969 to 1972 and ten years (1975–1985) as a staff sergeant in the US Marine Corps Reserves in B Company, 8th Tank Battalion located in Syracuse/Mattydale, New York. Leon, along with his wife Margaret (Peggy) of forty-six years, currently live in the village of Loudonville, New York, a suburb of Albany City. They have been parish members of the Christ Our Light (formerly St. Francis) Roman Catholic Church in Loudonville since 1990. Leon has served in multiple capacities in the parish over the years as a mass coordinator, lector, eucharistic minister, confirmation mentor and on the parish council. Peg taught in Catholic schools for over eight years at the elementary level and is currently the Secretary of the Altar Rosary Society.

Leon and Peg have raised three beautiful children, two boys (Larry and Michael) and one girl (Theresa), who are now full-fledged married adults with wonderful spouses (Erin, Taylor, and Jim (Van Duyne), respectively). Larry and Erin have blessed us with two wonderful grandchildren, Madeline and Lorelei, two balls of youthful energy and exhuberance that have brought much pleasure and laughter into our lives.

Retirement has afforded Leon with the unique opportunity to focus his spiritual heart's desire of seeking a more meaningful and deeper loving relationship with God—Father, Son, and Holy Spirit. This book, *A Spiritual Journey into Ecclesiastes* is his first in-depth effort at exploring his relationship with God. He hopes that this first effort will also allow for some deeper contemplation on each reader's part about their own spiritual relationship and life journey with God. It is his hope that this foray into spiritual contemplation will not be his or your last effort at seeking a deeper spiritual communion with the Triune God of heaven and earth. God bless you one and all. Amen.

CPSIA information can be obtained
at www.ICGtesting.com
Printed in the USA
LVHW030553030323
740789LV00003B/62